PROCLAMATION

LENT

**INTERPRETING
THE LESSONS OF
THE CHURCH YEAR**

THOMAS HOYT, JR.

**PROCLAMATION 5
SERIES B**

FORTRESS PRESS   MINNEAPOLIS

PROCLAMATION 5
Interpreting the Lessons of the Church Year
Series B, Lent

Cover and interior design: Spangler Design Team

Library of Congress Cataloging-in-Publication Data
(Revised for Ser. B, v. 1-4)

Proclamation 5.

    Contents: ser. A. [2] Epiphany / Pheme Perkins —
[etc.] — ser. B. [1] Advent/Christmas / William H.
Willimon — [2] Epiphany / David Rhoads — [3] Lent /
Thomas Hoyt, Jr. — [4] Holy Week / Walter Wink.
    1. Bible—Homiletical use. 2. Bible—Liturgical
lessons, English. I. Perkins, Pheme.
BS534.5.P765 1993   251   92-22973
ISBN 0-8006-4185-X (ser. B, Advent/Christmas)
ISBN 0-8006-4186-8 (ser. B, Epiphany)
ISBN 0-8006-4187-6 (ser. B, Lent)
ISBN 0-8006-4188-4 (ser. B, Holy Week)

Manufactured in the U.S.A.   AF 1-4187

97   96   95   94   93   1   2   3   4   5   6   7   8   9   10

CONTENTS

Preface

Lent is a special time in the church year. It signifies a time in which participants celebrate discipline of mind, body, attitude, and spirit in preparation for the work of ministry to oneself, God, and the community. This book is intended to serve as a basis for reflection on themes frequently encountered on the pilgrimage of life. Discussion of the biblical text offers an opportunity to reflect on Lenten themes based on lectionary readings while seeking to confront questions of our own day and time. While "new occasions teach new duties," we must always be cognizant of the foundations of our faith.

This book is intended for pastors and laypersons who want to go through a journey with the Scriptures. I give thanks to persons who have assisted me in preparation for this book. I am especially thankful for the assistance of Barbara Essex who offered invaluable homiletical input. I also thank the students at Hartford Seminary, Howard University, and the Interdenominational Theological Center who have helped refine some of the thoughts in this book. The input of those laypersons and ministers from many denominations, including my own, the Christian Methodist Episcopal Church, has been invaluable.

This book would not have been completed without the timely technical assistance of David Lott and Timothy Staveteig. The staff, faculty, and administration of Hartford Seminary have always offered assistance, and to them I offer thanks. To my wife, Ocie, who has been there for me in so many ways, I dedicate this book to you. My hope is that the work expended on this project will bear fruit for those who read it.

Introduction

Lent begins on Ash Wednesday and lasts for forty days, concluding with Easter Eve. Forty is a symbolic, biblical number. The numbers "four" and "forty" symbolize wholeness and completeness as in the four winds, the four seasons, the four corners of the earth, the four directions, and the four stages of life. There is a newness, a completion that emerges after a forty-day wilderness experience—persons are fortified and strengthened because adversity and temptation have made them strong.

Forty as a symbolic number can be seen in the forty-day wilderness journey of the children of Israel; the forty days in which Moses was on Mount Sinai receiving the law; and Jesus' forty days in the wilderness preparing for his ministry. This latter experience serves as a model for the Christian Lenten season. Ash Wednesday, the fortieth day before Easter, is our beginning point in this series of studies.

Ash Wednesday

Lutheran	Roman Catholic	Episcopal	Common Lectionary
Joel 2:12-19	Joel 2:12-18	Joel 2:1-2, 12-17	Joel 2:1-2, 12-17a
2 Cor. 5:20b—6:2	2 Cor. 5:20—6:2	2 Cor. 5:20b—6:10	2 Cor. 5:20b—6:2 (3-10)
Matt. 6:1-6, 16-21	Matt. 6:1-6, 16-18	Matt. 6:1-6, 16-21	Matt. 6:1-6, 16-21

FIRST LESSON: JOEL 2:1-2, 12-19

The book of Joel is a liturgically oriented prophetic book, probably used in the cultic celebration of the Jewish community. No concrete information concerning the prophet Joel exists in the book itself except his identification as the "son of Pethuel" (Joel 1:1). Since the dates of Joel's ministry cannot be known exactly, we can only say that this book appears to have been written in response to an impinging national catastrophe (2:27). Not even that tragedy, however, is pinpointed within the book itself. Conjecture is based on what Joel includes, references from earlier prophets, and what he excludes, such as any mention of the Assyrians or Babylonians.

Dates given for writing the book of Joel have varied from the late ninth century B.C.E. to the eighth century B.C.E., the years immediately preceding the fall of Jerusalem (597–587 B.C.E.), the time after the rebuilding of the temple (515–500), the end of the fifth century, or as late as the third century. Most scholars now conjecture on historical and linguistic grounds that Joel's ministry took place around 400 to 350 B.C.E.

The book of Joel announces the day of the Lord. In that day, according to traditional expectation, God would vindicate God's people, exalt them, give them power, and reward them with God's blessing. It is little wonder then that people did not want to hear the prophecy of Joel. He calls the people to repentance and for them to do the groundwork for the day, including fasting and enacting ceremonies of communal sorrow. This alone probably accounts for its selection as an Ash Wednesday text.

For Joel, as for other prophets, the day of the Lord is not to be coveted but rather to be feared. On the day of the Lord, Yahweh's own people would be judged as well as the nations (Isa. 2:4, 6-22); Amos warned that the day of Yahweh would be wrath, not vindication (Amos 5:18-20). Zephaniah announced universal destruction, yet offered hope for the humble righteous (Zeph. 1:2).

The blowing of the shofar, or the horn of the ram, issues an alarm of danger (vv. 1-2). One should stop and take notice, for something very important is about to take place. Judea is in danger of destruction. The day of the Lord signals judgment for a disobedient people. The time is short and the nation is in a state of emergency. In the same way, Ash Wednesday signals the call of the church to attention. It begins a six-week period of fasting, praying, and almsgiving in the spirit of repentance so that one might draw closer to God. This period is not for the individual alone but, as Joel will show, for the sake of community.

Judea is called to return and repent, with stipulations or requirements for that call (vv. 12-13a). The people are told that it is not too late to return to the Lord (v. 12), but they must do so with all their heart. The implication is that the people had at one time been in favor with God. They had been in a right covenant relationship with God. This is a relationship in which God, who had delivered them from bondage and led them through the wilderness to the promised land, promises to be their God and they God's people. Now God is aggrieved because God's people have been unfaithful to the covenant. They are now told to return, not with their half-hearted ritualistic gestures, but with their whole being.

"Rend your hearts and not your clothing" (v. 13). "Rend your hearts" is a communal call and recognizes that all the community is in need of *turning*. The Hebrew word for "turn" is *sub* and is frequently used in prophetic books. When used in the context of covenant community, it means to turn to God, or to return to God. They are to "tear their hearts." Since the Hebrew understanding of heart is the seat of will and emotion, to "tear the heart" seems to be an expression indicating the purging of corruption or evil from that seat.

Hard-hearted, Godless people are unwilling and/or unable to open themselves to God or others. When one's heart is torn, it becomes a receptacle able to receive love and concern. Indeed, Israel's heart has turned away from God, a closed-up vessel that needed to be reopened to God's grace and mercy. Repentance—a true re-turning to God—is possible and a requirement of the covenant relationship.

"Not your clothing" (v. 13)—the characteristic sign of repentance was tearing of clothing. This showed sincerity, honesty, fervency. This is like saying change your behavior through changing the seat of will and emotion, the heart. Don't give money for a hospital as a substitute for examining why you wish to give money for this cause. Don't half-heartedly send money to the inner city, but instead will to do the right thing whether you feel like doing it or not. That's what love is all about.

Verses 13b-14 issue a reiteration of God's call of repentance by the prophet. Joel is familiar with a God who has repented of intended judgment in the past. Perhaps if the people turn and repent, God will again forgive and relent in punishment. Joel believes this because he has read of a God who is gracious and merciful, slow to anger, and abounding in steadfast love (Ps. 103:8). Verse 13b explicitly states to whom they are to return. It is to their God, who is well known by what this God has done. Joel contends that it was *your* God who earned the right to be so called.

Joel begins to articulate why he calls God "your God." God is gracious, meaning grace has been bestowed upon Israel. Grace did not just start with Jesus. Grace was involved in telling Abraham to go out where he knew not and that he and his seed would be blessed. Grace was associated with providing for renewal of a covenant with Noah. Grace was involved in the escape of Israelite slaves from Egypt to the promised land. Grace helped an exiled southern kingdom to survive the Babylonian captivity and return to its own land. "God is gracious and merciful"—God is patient and faithful, giving mercy when wrath is deserved. If God decides that God will bless the people and keep back the punishment, it would be appropriate to celebrate that blessing through a sacrificial offering as epitomized by a grain and a drink offering (v. 14).

Verses 15-17a give prophetic stipulations urging the people of God to assemble as a community as a sign of their return to God. The "community" is defined in such a manner as to be inclusive: the elderly, the children, infants, and those about to create new families. The community respects everyone: the old, the young, and single persons! In modern times, there is a tendency to ostracize single persons because they do not fit the traditional mode of "family." This text, however, embraces all members of the community and makes them part of the congregation.

The means of this return of the community to God is through fasting, praying, and almsgiving. While the congregation is to gather and be sanctified, the priests are to earnestly pray for the people. Weeping is a sign of deep sincerity and authenticity. This was evident when Jesus wept upon learning that Lazarus had died and when Jesus wept over Jerusalem. Even in our own lives, the weeping prayer is deeper, more intense, more cathartic. It symbolizes a genuine opening of self to God. Ministers of God are called to weep and to pray for God's people.

The priests are to tell the people that they must return to the Lord through fasting (v. 15). The purpose of blowing the shofar is to get the attention of people and announce a national emergency. A national *fast must be sanctified*, an *assembly must be called*, and *people must be gathered*. Fasting means to go without food for a time so that one might properly reach within the self in order to be prepared to reach authentically out to others.

A fast was usually prescribed by Mosaic law in conjunction with celebration of the day of atonement, "at onement with God" (Lev. 16:29-31; 23:27). Persons could voluntarily practice fast days, except those proclaimed in the time of national emergency (Joel 2:15). Usually fasting is associated with mourning, a sign of penitence, attending to prayer, and preparing for reception of divine revelation. Not only is one called to make holy an event of repentance but one must make holy the *persons* participating in the event of repentance. Signs of repentance would indeed be mourning and weeping.

Two factors condition the fast: First, the whole community should be involved. Second, the urgency of the event of repentance is so immediate that not even those preparing for marriage should remain in their room. Everyone should gather, the aged, children, and infants.

The functionaries of God are to stand between the vestibule and altar, serving for the people as examples of repentance characterized by weeping. The priests, positioned as it were between the people and God, are not only called to *weep* but also to *speak* on behalf of the people words of mercy for their waywardness. They are to ask God to spare the people even though they deserve punishment. This is not to be done for their sakes alone. All the nations do not know or claim that Yahweh is God. Yahweh's reputation, therefore, is at stake. The worst fear of a priest is that God's elected people will be put to shame among the nations because of their disobedience (v. 17).

Since every nation had its God, the priest makes a plea to God to save them from punishment or shame, to save them from being cut off as a nation of status among other nations, and to save them from the humiliation of those who would surely say that Israel's God is not powerful, does not save, and is silent when people need that God the most. If the case is made by the priest that Yahweh must save in order to maintain Yahweh's name as one who is concerned about Yahweh's people and the nation's status, then the statement that God *became jealous* must mean that God became concerned about the land that God loved and wished to spare it and vindicate God's name among God's own people and in the sight of other nations.

To become *jealous for God's land* and to have *pity for God's people* signifies that God is about to do something. Jealousy and pity are emotions that erupt into actions. The author is consistent that emotions in God's being lead to action or behaviors. What are those behaviors? It can be argued that one runs because one is scared or one is scared because one runs. However we arrive at an answer, we must conclude that for Joel, God acts because God first has felt jealousy for the land and pity for the people (v. 18).

"Jealous" also connotes "zealous"—God has a zeal, an ardor for what is God's own! Perhaps God is reluctant to give over to destruction that which God has pronounced good. Throughout Israel's history with God, the foundation of the promise has rested on "the land." Thus, land carries significant theological weight. For people who were once a desperate band of nobodies, the land provides a base upon which they built identity and status among the nations. Without land, they are not a nation; without God they are not a people. God provides that which gives meaning: a name and a land.

Something happens in response to the fast and the intercession of the priest for the sake of God's name. These rebellious people are called to fast, repent, and thereby avoid God's punishment. They are God's people, the elected ones whom God's graciousness and mercy has girded. These are God's people who now, because of the priest's intercessory prayers on behalf of a fasting congregation, get a word from the Lord.

God promises instead of a punishment, prosperity (v. 19). God promises military victory for Israel instead of prisoners of war and consequently shame among the nations (v. 20). The people should fear no more, for the Lord has done marvelous things (v. 21). The message is: National repentance brings a day of the Lord that vindicates Judah/

Israel and serves as a time of salvation, restoring the nation's identity: God, land, and a name.

SECOND LESSON: 2 CORINTHIANS 5:20b—6:2

Scholars have generally seen from three to five separate letters in 2 Corinthians. Our scriptural texts fit into the so-called joyful letter of 2 Corinthians 1–9. The problems raised in chapters 10–13, the so-called severe letter, were apparently resolved by the time 2 Corinthians 1–9 was written. In this context of joy, Paul begins to reiterate the saving grace of God, to call for reconciliation to God, and to recount the high act of a sinless one dying for sinful people in order to effect the righteousness of God. The implication is that righteousness cannot be achieved or earned but merely imputed and accepted. It is God's action and our response must be a yes or no to that gift.

Paul is speaking to a Corinthian church that has gone through various phases of faith. Some are new converts who are vulnerable to problems confronting people in Corinth: divisions, problems of marriage, idolatry, disorder in worship, and spiritual gifts; quarrelling, boasting, litigation, and immorality. The content of 2 Corinthians outlines the following concerns: Chapters 1–7 deal mainly with comfort in affliction; chapters 8–9 deal mainly with the collection for Jerusalem; and chapters 10–13 mainly with vindication of the apostle Paul's apostolic authority.

Our text comes out of a discussion of the real source and power of the Christian ministry: the afflictions and sufferings of Christ. Since Jesus Christ has suffered great afflictions, the disciple should be ready to experience such also, for in them and through them the disciple feels the presence of God, turning these deadly afflictions into a glorious victory. Paul makes a personal appeal to them for mutual affection, and to separate themselves by avoiding marriage with non-Christians. Paul even rejoices in their repentance. He compares his sufferings with those of Christ and talks briefly about the resurrection of all believers (4:7-18; 5:1-10).

Second Corinthians addresses, among other things, the Corinthian attack on Paul's apostleship. Our lesson for today comes in the middle of Paul's defense of his apostleship. He says in chapter 3 that his work speaks for him and he needs no letter of recommendation. In chapter 4, apostles are to remain in the background and give all glory to God. In chapter 5, the heart of today's lesson, two undercurrents appear: the references to life after death and the doctrine of the atonement, reconciliation. Paul appeals to the Corinthians to be reconciled to God (2 Cor. 5:20). This admonition arose from Paul's concern for their alienation from him and their misunderstanding of his ministry (2 Cor. 1:23—6:13). Evidently, he expected that a renewal of their relationship with God on the basis of divine reconciliation in Christ would resolve the problems existing between humans.

The word *reconciliation* appears five times in 2 Corinthians 5:18-21, thus signifying one of Paul's most important theological statements. By dying on a cross Jesus became a sin offering for believers, effecting atonement, so that in Jesus we might become the righteousness of God (2 Cor. 5:21). "God was in Christ reconciling the world to himself" (v. 19).

In 5:18-20, the announcement is made in the preaching of the "message of reconciliation." This word announces what God has done in Jesus Christ so that it can become reality in every human life. Paul says that we are "ambassadors for Christ," meaning that we stand in the place of Christ. This implies that when this message is proclaimed it is not the voice of the preacher that is to be heard, but God's call and invitation to human beings to be reconciled to God.

Ambassadors in the Roman Empire represented the government to arrange terms of peace, determine the boundaries of new provinces, draw up constitutions, and so forth, all in the name of the one who sent them. The ambassadors were to assume the responsibility of bringing others into the family of the Roman Empire. Likewise, Paul saw himself and others who were reconciled as having the responsibility of bringing others into the reconciled family. That's why Paul admonished the Corinthians who were alienated from him to "be reconciled to God" (v. 20).

While all Christians must exercise this ministry in their own lives, Paul referred to those in his own ministry who were alienated from him and thus nullified the truth of the gospel. If one is reconciled to God through Christ, one's daily expressions of life should show this. If not, the Corinthians and any others who profess but do not practice reconciliation may be guilty of having received "the grace of God in vain" (6:1).

The lives of men and women who pay heed to the gospel thus will be reconciled to God through Christ's death. But a convert who goes against God's will discredits a minister's work. Nevertheless, the genuineness of the work of those in ministry is proven by the spiritual quality of their lives, the truth and force of their message, and their reaction to the sufferings with which they are afflicted. This is the way in which the true minister of God commends oneself to the attention of others who criticize one's ministry (5:11—6:10).

To hear with the ears is one thing, but to really hear with one's total being is another. Listening means to be attentive to another in a personal way. It means that one is attuned to the body language and what is not said as well as what is said. In psychology, it is said that one must listen with the third ear. Some may call this way of listening insightful listening or the discernment of the spirit. Whatever one names the listening event, one must conclude that it must entail real presence.

One cannot work on behalf of another without first listening. Without the ability to listen, one does not know the hurts, longings, or structural factors that prohibit real fulfillment, nor the reasons why people seek to escape the problems of life through artificial means. Listening, sometimes, is all that we can do. In fact, many who are going through difficulties only want and need someone to be there with a sympathetic ear. Listening can be salvific and healing.

Throughout Scripture, we find a God who listens. In anthropomorphic terms, Yahweh is a "God of hearing" who has challenged God's people to listen: "Hear, O Israel, the LORD your God is one" (the Shema); Jesus admonishes those who have ears yet don't hear. Listening and hearing are active rather than passive verbs. Our lives are to be active based on what we hear from God and from sisters and brothers who cry out to be heard and understood.

GOSPEL: MATTHEW 6:1-6, 16-21

Matthew's Gospel was directed toward the Jewish Christians and the Gentiles of Asia Minor. This Gospel thinks through the relation of Christianity to Judaism. After 70 C.E., the Pharisaism that Jesus knew became Rabbinic Judaism. With the destruction of the temple at Jerusalem, Judaism had to rethink its relationship to the worship of God. Transference of tradition passed from the hands of the Sadducees and the priestly aristocracy to the lay teachers of the law, the rabbis. Part of the rabbis' program was to consolidate their influence over other Jewish communities by squeezing out the Christians.

When Matthew wrote of Jesus' conflicts with the Pharisees, he was not simply recording the tradition of what Jesus said and did; he was telling the story to help his own congregation deal with the synagogue they knew. He blended the tradition with his own times. He had to ask, "Is Christianity the fulfillment of Judaism? Does Christianity represent the real point of Judaism that the synagogue was distorting?" Since Matthew's Gospel was written around 90 C.E., this situation in life seems to fit perfectly the character of Matthew's congregation.

Although an imminent expectation of the end of the age is maintained in Matthew, the necessary period of waiting required directions for individual and church. In the Matthean context, the resurrected Jesus gives a charge to his disciples. They are sent to do mission, making disciples of all nations, baptizing, and teaching. The risen Jesus commands the disciples to remember his earthly teachings and to make those teachings part of their missionary work (Matt. 28:19-20). This shows us how Matthew views his own work. He sees himself as a participant in the universal mission of the church with the ethical implications of being in the reign of God.

Verses 1-6 and 16-18 are part of the thematic discussion in 6:1-18 that revolve around three basic features of Judaism: almsgiving, fasting, and prayer. Almsgiving, or giving money to the poor, was one of several ways commanded in the Old Testament to provide for the poor and needy (See Deut. 15:7, 9, 11; Prov. 14:21; Isa. 58:7). By the second century B.C.E., almsgiving was considered one of the highest expressions of righteousness that benefited both the giver and the receiver. In fact, after the destruction of the temple and of the sacrificial system, almsgiving was considered by some as atonement for sin. While Jesus warns against giving to be seen, he still assumes the continuation of charity mandated by Judaism.

The Nature of the Sermon on the Mount. The Sermon has been variously assessed by scholars. Some think it presupposes an "interim ethic" (see Albert Schweitzer, *The Mystery of the Kingdom of God: The Secret of Jesus' Messiahship and Passion,* trans. Walter Lowrie [London: A. & C. Black, 1925]), which makes demands in light of the impending day of judgment. Others see the sermon as emphasizing an impossible ethic that convicts of sin and thus makes one rely solely on the grace of God. One common interpretation is that the sermon provides useful material for setting up a political or social program. None of these views is entirely satisfactory. They either ignore the original intent of the sayings in the Sermon on the basis of a Pauline model, or make too radical a thoroughgoing eschatological assertion.

In spite of sin, death, and evil, the Sermon on the Mount affirms the dawning of the new age and the demand for a new behavior. With Jesus' coming, a transformation of the world has transpired. The Sermon is not a new law in the traditional sense, but contains symptoms and signs pointing to the dawning of a new age. Much of the material in Matthew, including the Gospel reading for Ash Wednesday, deals with Jewish law and practices (Matt. 5:17—6:18).

Literary Concerns.   Contextually, Matthew 6:2-4 is part of a combination of short sayings on alms, prayer, and fasting, all of which are introduced (Matt. 6:2, 5, 16) and concluded (Matt. 6:4, 6, 18) in parallel formulas. Substantively, they illustrate the primacy of motive in piety and contrast deeds done to achieve the approval of human beings and those done to receive the reward of God. Matthew has a tendency to group his material under a common theme which, in the case of the material for today's Gospel lesson, is Jewish piety: 6:2-4 (almsgiving); 6:5-6 (prayer); 6:7-8 (warning against praying like Gentiles); 6:9-14 (Lord's Prayer); 6:14-15 (expression of the forgiveness found in the Lord's Prayer); and 6:16-18 (fasting).

Our text is presented in the context of Jesus' judgment upon those guilty of false piety (6:1-18). The behavior demanded of disciples in Matthew is designated as righteousness (6:1, 21). In the Sermon on the Mount, Jesus provides the proper interpretation of the Torah (especially 5:21-48), and of the three basic forms of piety: alms, prayer, and fasting (Matt. 6:1-18). Matthew shows that Jesus did not come to do away with the Scripture but to fulfill it, and has him say so as well (Matt. 5:17-19). For Matthew, the righteousness required by God has been stated in the Torah and has been rightly interpreted by Jesus' words and deeds.

Almsgiving was considered especially virtuous among first-century Jews. Its kinship to mercy indicates the idea that alms was a primary means of enacting gracious concern. It would have been natural, therefore, for Jesus to have spoken of alms. Almsgiving especially became a sign of sacrifice after the destruction of the temple in 70 C.E. The New Testament especially stresses almsgiving as a sign of righteousness. Matthew gives short, pithy sayings emphasizing that these gifts are to

15

be offered with sincerity and should not be used to evoke the praise of others (Matt. 6:1-4).

Matthew 6:1 states the theme: "Beware of practicing your piety before others in order to be seen by them; for then you have no reward from your Father in heaven." Jesus, therefore, warned against parading one's generosity. "Sound a trumpet" (Matt. 6:2) was figurative language dramatizing the hypocritical practice of publicizing benefactions. In Joel, sounding a trumpet was an attention-getting device intended to call the nation to attention. Here trumpet-blowing is a negative invoked against self-seeking almsgiving. Such trumpet-blowing received a reward, but it involved (1) the praise of human beings and (2) payment in full. The verb *apegousin* appeared in the papyri materials as a commercial formula for a receipt indicating payment in full. The kingdom, on the other hand, demanded secret alms if the disciple was tempted toward public show (Matt. 6:3). Anonymous alms not done for reward evoke God's reward, the content of which is not stated by Jesus.

Already, before the time of Jesus, giving alms in secret was a Jewish prescription. This was an injunction to protect the self-respect of the recipient. Among some in the rabbinic order, ostentatious almsgiving was even viewed as evil. Giving to be seen and praised by others is wrong in motivation.

Those who wanted to impress others with their piety would fast in private and then go public with a somber and unwashed face. The admonition in Matthew 6:16-18 against fasting for show evidently regards private rather than public fasting. Strict Pharisees were known to fast twice a week (Luke 18:12). Since the public fast on the Day of Atonement required that one abstain from washing and anointing, we know that this fast was a private one. Only private fasting would allow one to call attention to oneself by not washing or being anointed (6:16-18). The insincere attracted attention to themselves by engaging in private fasts, following the mandates of the public fasts of the atonement. Jesus, on the other hand, advised his followers to fast but to look fresh. "Put oil on your head and wash your face." In other words, they are to have a normal appearance.

Matthew 6:19-21 admonishes followers of Jesus to get their priorities right. Because wealth is temporary, Jesus, according to Matthew, demanded renunciation of it. Stated negatively, the command was expressed, "Do not lay up for yourselves treasures on earth" (Matt. 6:19), meaning that one should not devote oneself to prioritizing one's life around purely earthly matters that do not reach out to others. This Palestinian idiom is paralleled more explicitly in Luke 12:33: "Sell your possessions, and give alms." For Matthew's context, heavenly treasures are preferable to earthly ones. From a positive perspective, Jesus exclaimed, "Store up for yourselves treasures in heaven" (Matt. 6:20), by which he probably meant the practice of self-giving deeds.

As Matthew 6:21 (par. Luke 12:34) verifies, the demand is not ascetic, for the problem is not *possession* of earthly goods but *commitment* to them. It is the fallacy of treating transient realities with an estimation of ultimacy. Making absolute that which is nonabsolute is illogical, since it offers only false hope while, at the same time, it prevents one from affirming true security.

Sometimes, persons attempt to bring stability and security by accumulating things. They become so obsessed with driving the "right" car, wearing the "right clothes," being seen in the "right" places with the "right" people, that they lose sight of what is really important. Some think that their careers and accomplishments are more important than developing quality meaningful relationships with God and others. We are challenged to think deeply about what is of most value to us— individually and as a church. To squander life on things and to miss the blessings of relationships is sinful and shows a lack of stewardship.

Three reasons are given for prioritizing one's life. First, earthly treasures wear out (rust and moth). Second, earthly treasures can be stolen (thieves). Third, one's heart is centered on that which governs one's life. Where the heart is, there is one's treasure.

The Jewish community is cautioned against hypocrisy. It is a caution against the sin of familiarity. When ritual becomes routine and mechanical, the real meaning of one's behavior becomes pretentious. Jesus seems to challenge the leaders among the Jews to be real and not counterfeit. When a husband or wife can sing, "I've become accustomed to your face," in a way that does not vibrate with warmth, appreciation, or love, the marriage is dead. If the Declaration of Independence repeats consistently, "We hold these truths to be self-evident, that all men are created equal, that they are endowed by their creator with certain unalienable rights, that among these are life, liberty, and the pursuit of happiness," but those who repeat such words consistently do not even try to uphold them, the claims sound counterfeit. Being real, not hypocritical, in one's giving, praying, and fasting, is a call to authenticity.

First Sunday in Lent

Lutheran	Roman Catholic	Episcopal	Common Lectionary
Gen. 22:1-18	Gen. 9:8-15	Gen. 9:8-17	Gen. 9:8-17
Rom. 8:31-39	1 Peter 3:18-22	1 Peter 3:18-22	1 Peter 3:18-22
Mark 1:12-15	Mark 1:12-15	Mark 1:9-13	Mark 1:9-15

FIRST LESSON: GENESIS 22:1-18

This story of Abraham and Isaac occurs in the land of the Philistines in a place called Beer-sheba and recounts an event in Isaac's adolescence. This text is concerned with Abraham's response to God's instructions to make a sacrifice of his son Isaac (22:1-2). Isaac was very important to Abraham, not only because he had satisfied the social pressures for offspring, but also because he was the lifeline through whom all nations would be blessed (Gen. 12:2; 17:2, 5, 6, 9, 10, 21; 21:12). Abraham's own hopes and plans were connected with what he perceived God had asked of him. Yet, in obedience to God's instructions, he was willing to deny himself his own hopes for future satisfaction and joy.

The act of child sacrifice in order to win the favor of a god was a common practice of people throughout the Fertile Crescent. Abraham now came to the conclusion that God required of him the sacrifice of what was most precious to him, his son Isaac. His faith in God had been tested over and over in the many years of wandering following God's call. Now his faith confronted the highest test. Although God had given him a son and promised to bless his descendants, God's promise now seemed to be broken.

The idea of the testing of God is a difficult theological concept and one that has caused much pain and anguish for many who seek to do God's will. For some, it makes God seem tentative and unsure about the loyalty and commitment of those whom God has chosen. Perhaps this idea of testing fits in with the biblical notion that God demands unconditional acceptance of those whom God has chosen to do God's will.

The idea of testing also sets the stage for dualistic thinking, as in Job and Satan (both with Job and Jesus). It is very easy for people to say all their trials and tribulations are God's ways of testing them, which certainly is not the case. To affirm that God is testing one when one cannot understand the ramifications of one's life could be the attempt of human beings to understand the mysteries of life.

In Genesis 22:3-13, 15-18, Abraham is put to the test. He is motivated to obey God's command and respond in faith, in spite of his lack of understanding of the ways of God. He trusts God and is prepared to obey God even if it means giving up what is most precious to him. As he is about to sacrifice his son, he realizes as clearly as if a messenger from heaven had proclaimed it, that God did not want the death of his son, but a demonstration of Abraham's trust. At the crucial moment when Isaac lay bound and Abraham lifts the knife to kill him, the angel of God appears and prevents Abraham from carrying out the commanded sacrifice.

A ram, which had become entangled in the bushes, suddenly appears, and is offered in Isaac's place. The ram in the bush is revealed only after Abraham's faith has been tested. Abraham names that place *Jehovah-jireh*—"The Lord will provide" (vv. 13-14). The writer even repeats that God gives Abraham more promises of abundance. The angel of the Lord renews the promise to Abraham that the Lord will bless Abraham and will greatly multiply his descendants. The story contends that Abraham's willingness to do God's will even though denying his own, eventuates in a satisfaction that Abraham could never have imagined.

This is a strange story that some have called an etiological narrative, a story told to explain why something is the way it is. In this case, the story is an explanation of the reason human sacrifice is not practiced in Israel as in neighboring countries. Israel is devoted to her God to the extent that if human sacrifice were required, obedience would be the order of the day. Yet the story says that Israel's God does not demand such loyalty or sacrifice. A concomitant meaning is that God demands something of us that our reason cannot understand. Although our human sensibilities and the context of the cross may cause us to contend that the sacrifice of one's children is not to be advocated, we can say that God may call us to do and be that which we may find offensive to our reason. Circumstances, convictions, and the discernment of the Holy Spirit will determine the bounds of our obedience to the will of God.

In our so-called sophisticated civilization, many have raised a question about the propriety of Abraham's belief and willingness to offer his son as a sacrifice because he believed that this was what God willed. We may have to raise the question: Are we so much different from the ancient belief of sacrifice? Do we not sacrifice our young men and women on the altar of war against other countries? Do we not sacrifice many of our young persons in the name of protecting our country's honor? Do we not sacrifice many of our young men and women on the altar of greed, materialism, and militarism? Do we not sacrifice our young on the altar of drugs, crime, illiteracy, and premature parenting? With fervor and zeal fathers have proudly sent their sons to die sacrificially for what the fathers believed were worthwhile causes. We also are often drawn more into God's love and purposes by denying self with sacrifices that we sometimes do not understand. It is clear that God's will and purposes—or simply God's glory—should be supreme over our lives.

Behind these sacrifices is the idea that we know better than God what is needed. We rush in with humanly devised solutions as if every problem has a technological or rational answer. Many answers to our problems do come from rational sources. On our own, however, we can never know enough to make genuinely wise choices and decisions. One who is willing to wait on the Lord, to listen to that still, small voice, to discern the will of God, is one who lives triumphantly. Triumph is less about being victorious and more about being faithful!

ALTERNATIVE FIRST LESSON: GENESIS 9:8-15

In life there is blessing and disaster. Disaster always threatens to pervade the creation. The story of Noah begins with disaster and chaos, reminiscent of the creation story in Genesis 1 and the new creation in Genesis 6–9. The earth was created out of chaos, water, and the moving of the primeval ocean. In the story of the flood, the waters foreshadow a cosmic catastrophe that will return the earth once again to watery chaos. In the first creation story, *ruach*—God's breath, Spirit, or wind—hovered over the chaos, pushing back the waters so that land, animals, and human beings could grow and be fruitful. The new creation after the flood portrays the renewal of the earth, when God's wind/Spirit/breath blows the waters aside to make room again for replenishing the plants, animals, and all living beings. The Noah story is based on the

Creator's covenant that opens up a future for human beings and the world.

Between the two creations, the created order lies in danger. The catastrophe of the flood was not simply a natural calamity, nor was it an unmotivated act of God. Corruption had so infected the earth that God's judgment came upon it to cleanse the earth and to make a new beginning. The stories present violence as a disease, contaminating all living creatures who live in the same household of this earth (Gen. 6:11). The flood is the climax of earlier events: Adam and Eve had rebelled against God and been expelled from the Garden of Eden (Gen. 3:24); Cain had polluted the earth with the blood of his murdered brother (Gen. 4:9-10); Lamech had boasted of revenge brought on by his lust for power (Gen. 4:23-24).

We could easily add stories of our own. Violence begets violence, and because it cannot be confined or contained, it affects the entire created order, polluting the environment. The story of the flood shows how power corrupts if we misuse our freedom. Our actions have consequences. We cannot violate the created order without bringing severe penalties upon our world. We have the power to pollute the environment, to kill and maim others, to destroy the world with our nuclear weapons. We threaten the earth with a return to chaos. Noah's story is our story. Nevertheless, now as then, the Creator remains committed unconditionally to creation and blessing.

God stands at the crossroads of human history, assisting us to remember all the generations of covenant relationship, calling us always to affirm creation and not chaos. Our Maker seeks to move our history from the brink of disaster into a new creation, where there is a reordering of relationships between human beings and our environment. Affirming our potential to open our eyes and see, to repent and turn in a new direction, God calls us to become committed unconditionally to creation.

This reading tells of the covenant that God made with Noah after the flood, a promise that God would never again destroy the earth by flood (Gen. 9:8-15). In reality, this covenant is made with all flesh. God brings humankind into covenant relationship at precisely the point where we are in relationship with all the earth, including plants, animals, and human beings together. While having dominion over all the created order, humankind is reminded that dominion means stewardship, not domination. We are under the sovereignty and judgment of God. The covenant with Noah indicates a reverence and appreciation for all of life. Pollution of the earth is both a violation of the covenant with Noah and a disrespect for others.

The covenant is made between God and "every living creature for all generations," and its sign is to be the rainbow, a reminder for all times of God's promise. This is appropriate as a sign since it is a natural presence in the sky after a storm. The rainbow symbolizes the promise of hope in the presence of disaster and the potential for new creation. It is significant that the rainbow is made the sign of this covenant because the Hebrew word for bow quite literally refers to a weapon of war. Bolts of lightning were considered God's arrows, shot from God's bow (Ps. 7:12-13). Thus, that which was usually associated with war and divine judgment becomes the very sign of mercy. The symbol holds together God's judgment upon acts of violence of all kinds with God's grace that provides life with blessing and promise. The Noahic covenant is an everlasting covenant between God and all flesh. It is remembered and renewed each time we see the rainbow in the clouds (9:16). The Noahic covenant is unconditional, universal, and perpetual. The flood is already understood in the New Testament as a type of baptism.

SECOND LESSON: ROMANS 8:31-39

The hymn in Romans 8:31-39 celebrates the certainty of hope; grounded in God's electing grace, hope is confirmed in the resurrection of Jesus. Suffering, threats, powers, not even death itself can separate God's community from God. Romans 1–8 has been leading up to the climax of this triumphant hymn. The church is God's beloved people, Gentile as well as Jew; the faith of Abraham and God's promises to him are confirmed; the old age is being done away with, a new age has dawned upon a new community composed of Abraham's descendants among both the Jews and Gentiles. Nothing can prevent the completion of that which God has already begun in history.

It is the power of the Spirit of God that sustains those in tribulation and intercedes on their behalf (8:22-27). Paul is confident that nothing in the cosmos can cast believers away from the love of God. "Neither death, nor life, nor angels, nor rulers, nor things present, nor things to come, nor powers, nor heights, nor depth, nor anything else in all creation will be able to separate us from the love of God in Christ Jesus our Lord" (8:39). The one who is "in Christ" is not subject to death, sin, flesh, or the law, but lives in the Spirit assured of the present peace and future hope of complete redemption as children of God.

Romans 8:26-39 affirms the expectation that God will bring this fulfillment. God will do it in God's way, since persons of faith do not even know how to pray for that fulfillment. Being filled with the Spirit, Christians know that by the guarantee which the Spirit gives that the fulfillment is in the power of the One who predestines and glorifies.

The promises of God that give rise to hope are the foundation of our faith. When all seems lost, when destruction and chaos threaten, it is our hope that sustains and encourages us. What is most powerful about this is that nothing can sever the relationship between God and the faithful, sincere person. Despite outward appearances, in the face of overwhelming odds, we are able to hold on, to stand on God's promises. Through all circumstances, we can depend upon God's Word and trust Christ.

ALTERNATIVE SECOND LESSON: 1 PETER 3:18-22

Internal evidence of 1 Peter suggests that the situation of its readers is one of persecution. We have problems, however, determining the date of this letter and the persons inflicting persecution. In the first place, the suffering of the addressees does not seem to be the same throughout the letter. In 1:6, 2:20, 3:14-17, suffering is only a possibility; but in 4:12, 14, 19, the readers are already experiencing persecution. If one adds to those factors the doxology in 4:11 and the concrete address of 4:12ff., one derives a theory of diverse origins of 1:3—4:11 and 4:12—5:14. Different scholars have interpreted this data in various ways.

Some see 1:3—4:11 as a baptismal sermon put in the framework of a letter, including an exhortation by the same author. Others see the writing as two letters, one to those not yet persecuted and another to those under persecution. The general conclusion now widely accepted among scholars is that the early part of the writing is based on a baptismal homily the author habitually used. Now, during a time of actual persecution, this sermon becomes a call to young Christian communities to persevere on the basis of the gift of baptism and the eschatologically grounded universal necessity of suffering, a sign of the last days and therefore a reason for joy (4:7, 12; 5:6-10). This view has its roots in Judaism and deals with the Christian's justification in

Christ's suffering (4:13). This is reminiscent of Paul. The latter portion of the letter was added to adapt the whole letter for circulation among oppressed Christians in need of such comfort and encouragement.

First Peter 1:18-21 is considered one of the three christological hymnic fragments in this letter (the other two are 2:21-25 and 3:18-20). Here one detects the following emphases concerning who Jesus is: the eternal Christ, the incarnate Christ, the suffering Christ, the crucified Christ, the risen Christ, the glorified Christ, the redeeming Christ, and the sinless Christ.

First Peter 3:13—4:6 is concerned with the manner in which persecuted Christians should live on the basis of the hope Peter has delineated in 2:11—4:11. They are exhorted to be confident as they face persecutions. The practice of goodness will emerge victorious over unjust suffering. This exhortation is supported by Isaiah 8:11-15, quoted in verse 14b (3:13-17). The writer appeals to the passion and resurrection of Christ affirmed in their baptism as a model for their own courage in suffering. Through unjust suffering, Christ's death saved us. Unmerited suffering for others on the part of one who knew no sin and deserved no death should evoke reverence for Christ as Lord.

In 3:18, Peter begins to again remind Christians of the example of patient suffering they have in Christ. His statement develops into the most difficult in this letter. Essentially, in 3:18-22, the author presents different elements of a baptismal credo that emphasize the death of Christ in the flesh which has made believers alive in the Spirit (3:18); Christ's descent into hell where he preached (3:19); movement into discussion of baptism and then Christ's resurrection (3:21); and Christ's sitting at the right hand of God with authority over the powers (3:22). The topics are so loosely related that we could study each of them separately.

It is difficult to interpret the meaning of the descent of Christ into hell (3:19). Here and in 4:6, the statement "the gospel was proclaimed even to the dead" has no equivalent elsewhere in the New Testament. It may mean that just as the heavenly powers were subject to the ascended Christ (3:22), so the descended Christ had to notify the fallen angels of their subjection to the power of Christ (cf. Eph. 1:21f.; Col. 2:2:15).

Seeking to show the far-reaching love of God in Christ, the author remembers those who rebelled against the Almighty before the flood (3:20). The saving of the eight persons of Noah's household (including

Noah, his wife, his three sons, and their wives) during the flood has a counterpart in Christian baptism. As Noah's family was saved from the flood by the buoyancy of the water that held up the ark and destroyed the evil ones, so the baptized person passes safely through the waters that bury one's sins enabling the believer to find new life in Christ (3:20b-21). Baptism is therefore more than a washing with water, but involves "an appeal to God for a good conscience, through the resurrection of Jesus Christ" (3:21). This suggests that the baptismal ritual involved an act of covenanting with God on the part of the person being baptized.

It is God who through the cross and resurrection of Jesus has subjugated the powers (3:22). This means that the exalted Lord's authority over powers has made the baptized believer's life pregnant with possibilities.

There are unlimited possibilities for the baptized believer who is willing to live in the covenant made with Noah and all humanity that affirms the eternal presence and care of God. Just as Jesus struggled in the wilderness and came out victoriously fortified for mission, so can we. We need only realize that we must appropriate through faith the authority which has already been given through Christ's victory over the evil forces as 1 Peter has shown. The temptation account in Mark depicts the struggle that Jesus had to confront in preparation for ministry.

GOSPEL: MARK 1:12-15

The Temptation and Ministry. Mark's account of Jesus' temptation was chiefly written for the non-Jewish (Gentile) population of Rome and its empire. It is the shortest temptation account of the Synoptics. The author's intention for writing the Gospel is to depict primarily the historic significance of Jesus' message and ministry.

Mark does not have a long prologue as do Matthew, Luke, and John. Mark's Gospel begins with a brief preface (1:1), followed by the ministry and message of John (1:2-8). After the summary statement of John's activity, his designated role in the baptism of Jesus is reported (1:9-11). These verses, along with our verses for today (1:12-15), constitute the brief prologue to Mark's Gospel. In fact, the prologue to Mark ends with the temptation of Jesus.

25

Mark clearly connects the temptation with the baptism. The opening of the sky at Jesus' baptism (1:10) answers Isaiah's plea for the heavens to open and rain down messianic salvation (64:1). The quotation from Psalm 2:7, "You are my Son, the beloved" (1:11), is prophetic of the resurrection of Jesus Christ, the Son of God (1:1). Jesus fulfills John's announcement of approaching salvation.

The apocalyptic picture of Jesus' ministry is shown in verse 6 with the literary allusion to Elijah, whose return was expected prior to God's salvific intervention. It also provides the essential scenario for the baptism and temptation episodes. As Jesus emerges from the water, the sky is rent in two. The Spirit like a dove descends. A voice comes from the heavens (1:10-11). Like Mark, all three Gospels show the presence of God at the baptism of Jesus.

The testing accounts differ among the Gospels (Mark 1:12-21; Matt. 4:1-11; Luke 4:1-13). With sustained intensity, Mark and Matthew suggest that Jesus was compelled to go into the desert by the Spirit. Mark 1:12 reads, "The Spirit immediately drove him out into the desert." The desert is the habitat of the demonic world, the traditional place of evil forces. The desert is also the place of preparation for the revelation of God's salvific plan. The wilderness of Judea thus provides the setting for John's ministry and the meeting of the forces of evil with God's beloved Son.

In contrast, the Lukan version reads, "Jesus full of the Holy Spirit returned and was led by the Spirit into the desert." Luke is not satisfied with the Old Testament idea of the Spirit seizing a person. He pictures Jesus going into the desert under the inspiration of the Holy Spirit, as an agent "in," not "by," the Spirit. In all of the Synoptics (Matthew, Mark, and Luke), the moment of action had come. Jesus had to determine the nature and method of his mission. It was testing time.

Just as the forty days of Jesus in the wasteland recalls the forty years of the Israelite exodus, so also Jesus' baptism evokes the memory of their crossing of the Red Sea. Here John prepares the way for Jesus; here also Jesus prepares himself for his own way.

God's Son is tested. Mark names the tester "Satan" (Mark 1:13). In the book of Job, "Satan" was an accuser of human beings, a figure similar to a prosecuting attorney. He was one of God's angels, not a being who had set himself up in opposition to God.

Pre-exilic Yahwism contended so intently for God's absolute rulership that even evil was considered to be sent by God. Yahweh, for example, hardened Pharaoh's heart against Moses' plea. Under the influence of the Persian study of angels, Jewish writings during the two centuries prior to the birth of Jesus began to use the figure of Satan to account for the existence of evil in the world. "The Satan," God's prosecuting attorney who brought accusations against humankind, seemed so much in opposition to humans that it was a natural evolution of thought to begin depicting him as opposed to God also.

By New Testament times, as in Matthew and Luke, Satan was thought of as the lord of all that opposed God. Satan appealed to the "evil heart" in human beings, luring them from obedience to God. Yet it was impossible for Judaism to accept an ultimate dualism—a situation in which God and Satan were equally powerful figures, Satan being truly independent from God. Satan remains, therefore, a creature. His power is great, but limited. He holds sway over the present age, but he will be defeated and destroyed when the age of the reign of God begins. In the desert, Mark seems to depict the beginning battle with Satan and the forces of evil (v. 13—"wild beasts").

Although all three Gospels make use of Deuteronomy, each has its own nuance. Mark has Jesus rehearse the exodus experience of Israel in the desert in which the people are tested (Deut. 8:2). The difference is that as the "true Israel," Jesus relived the wilderness experience without yielding to the testing, while the Israel of old failed. Thus Mark used the Deuteronomic tradition to make his theological point.

The Gospels show similarities and differences. Matthew, for example, pictures Jesus upon the "high mountain" (Matt. 4:8, cf. Deut. 34:1-4). This parallels the tradition of Moses who gave the law on Mount Sinai. Matthew adds "forty nights" to the fast of "forty days" in order to relate more closely Jesus' fast to that of Moses (Matt. 4:2, Deut. 9:9, 18). Luke's version of the temptation experience does not include the combination "forty days and forty nights," but only mentions "forty days," signifying a "long time." His version omits the "high mountain" (Matt. 4:8); "He was with the wild beasts" (Mark 1:13); and "the angels waiting on him" (Matt. 4:11; Mark 1:13). These omissions related to the purposes and audience of each author.

Luke, like the other Gospels, uses the book of Deuteronomy as a fulcrum to lift up the essential theological points of the testing experiences. The book of Deuteronomy, one may surmise, must have been the popular scriptural book of the early apostolic church. In fact,

27

the three responses to the devil's testing are from Deuteronomy (Deut. 8:3; 6:13; 6:16).

Luke and Matthew's order of the temptation accounts are parallel, except Luke has the mountain temptation second and the temple temptation third. This ordering of material fits well into the theological schema of the writer. He wants important events to center around the temple.

In the first temptation, Jesus' tester urges him to turn a *stone* into bread. This is more of a personal testing, whereas in Matthew, the test is to turn *stones* into loaves. The suggestion is that Matthew pictures in Jesus all of Israel being tempted. In both accounts, Jesus is being asked to fit into the image of a kingly messiah and ignore the suffering servant role. Forget about the cross and think more about the glory that will be derived from feeding hungry people. Give food to the poor, down-trodden Palestinians, and the masses will truly listen. After all, one expectation of the Messiah was for someone to relieve their economic condition.

Jesus knew, however, that food for the stomach alone would not suffice. "Man [a human being] does not live on bread alone" (Deut. 8:3). This does not mean that bread is not necessary, but that it is not enough. There must be food for the soul, which material gifts cannot satisfy. Only God and God's Word can. This first temptation concerns the welfare of the body and soul, or the whole person.

In the second testing experience (depending on which Gospel one uses), the tempter causes the kingdoms of the world to pass before Jesus, and promises them to him in exchange for his worship. Luke, unlike Matthew, makes no mention of the mountain from which he could see all the kingdoms of the world. Evidently, this testing story describes an inward spirit, not an external event. There are no high mountains anywhere from which all of the kingdoms of the world are visible.

The tempter is in effect offering Jesus political power. He is offering what many claim and wish to possess: dominion, power, and authority. Whatever may be the historical veracity of this narrative, this is a fact, which can be followed throughout the Gospels, that Jesus viewed as a satanic temptation the zealot concept of Messiah (as one who would overthrow the governmental powers by force).

This temptation stemmed from at least two very different concepts of the Messiah that existed in Judaism during the time of Jesus.

According to the popular one, the Messiah would be a victorious warrior, who, as king upon earth, would establish a powerful kingdom of Israel through which God would rule over the world. Concretely, this temptation would mean that Jesus would consent to be a political leader, around whom people could rally against Roman power.

According to the other concept of messiah, advocated by small groups, the reign of God would be realized in a cosmic framework. The framework would be beyond earthly circumstances and would be ushered in by one like the "Son of man" of the book of Daniel and the apocryphal apocalypses, who would come "on the clouds of heaven."

Jesus probably did not regard himself as a political messiah, but, rather, as the "Son of man." He was at the same time conscious of fulfilling in his person the mission of the suffering servant spoken of by Deutero-Isaiah. In this temptation, Jesus rejects the method of bringing in the reign of God through the game of political intrigue backed by military force. The tempter was proposing that Jesus should use satanic power to further God's end. Jesus' reply was: "You shall worship the LORD your God, and him only shall you serve" (Deut. 6:13). God is God and God alone must be served.

In the third temptation, depending again on which Gospel is followed, the tempter suggests that, instead of using bread or politics as a bait for followers, Jesus should instead use his religion, by starring as a wonder-worker. He should leap from the pinnacle of the temple, satisfied that he would land unharmed four hundred-and-fifty feet below in the Kidron Valley. The tempter even quoted Scripture (Ps. 91:11-12), which promised that God would protect his own from disaster (Luke 4:11). People admire novelty and sensationalism. If he would do the sensational, he might win followers immediately for the kingdom. Jesus refused this demand for a sign because this was not the way of trust. Spectacular proof of his messianic calling would not lead to repentance, but marvel. When miracles ran out, people were prone to pull away. Jesus therefore said, "You shall not tempt the LORD your God" (Deut. 6:16).

Jesus, in these temptations, has refused the type of messiahship that would lead to a worship of any power other than God. He refuses to conform to the people's expectation of a messiah. He wishes to be a Messiah in obedience to God's will, not theirs.

In all three Gospels, Jesus is portrayed as victorious in that he completely commits himself to God. He would not be a political messiah. He would not be a sensational miracle worker. He would speak and act for God, whose reign is of the Spirit and not the sword.

In 1:14-15, Mark gives a summary, announcing the beginning of Jesus' public ministry. He reports the arrest of John. He suggests to his audience that they must repent—radically change their lives—believe in the work and person of the crucified and risen Christ, and participate in the reign of God that has come near.

The three temptations of Jesus in Matthew and Luke and the report in Mark that Jesus was tempted show that anyone who begins a mission must confront certain tests which others will impose. One may dare say that the three temptations in Matthew and Luke are mere summaries of a lifetime of testings in the life of Jesus.

Those who try to prove themselves on the basis of others' expectations will end up nullifying their own right to their unique contributions. If one feels called to a task, one should engage faithfully in that mission regardless of the obstacles and differences with others. A woman felt called to the ordained ministry, but her pastor felt that her calling did not correspond with his spirit. He thus denied that God had so called her and refused to assist in working with her. Must she give up on her dream and mission?

A boy is offered alcohol or drugs. He wants to be a part of the "in" crowd but he has been taught that this is not the way to treat the body nor the mind. "Prove you are a man—on our terms"—that is a constant temptation of youth. A young woman is asked to violate her sexual mores by a young man whom she loves. Should she "give in" and do what is the popular thing to do or must she seek to be loyal to the royal within her? A person is being treated unfairly on the job. Is it best to keep quiet and maintain one's own job or must one speak out in the face of oppressive forces? In a thousand ways, we all are confronted with the testing of our faith as we do God's will. In this period of Lent we are called to an overcoming faith as we seek to do ministry.

Dr. Franklyn Richardson, Executive Director of National Baptist Convention U.S.A., Inc., delivered a sermon in Hartford, Connecticut, to a Hartford Seminary graduating class in which he stated that we need to have "faith that defies context." Lent is a time to rethink, re-assess our personal faith and mission, and get fortified for the journey. It is a time of reflection on what is important and about what we ought to be doing if we are to be faithful disciples.

Just as Jesus went to the wilderness with God, and came out with God, so must we. Just as Jesus was tested and emerged confirmed, so can we be. Just as Jesus was waited on by angels, so will we be.

Second Sunday in Lent

Lutheran	Roman Catholic	Episcopal	Common Lectionary
Gen. 28:10-17	Gen. 22:1-2, 9a, 10-13, 15-18	Gen. 22:1-14	Gen. 17:1-10, 15-19
Rom. 5:1-11	Rom. 8:31b-34	Rom. 8:31-39	Rom. 4:16-25
Mark 8:31-38	Mark 9:2-10	Mark 8:31-38	Mark 8:31-38 or Mark 9:1-9

FIRST LESSON: GENESIS 28:10-17

(For Gen. 22:1-18, see First Sunday of Lent)

The story of God and Jacob at Bethel is probably an insertion into the Jacob/Esau stories. Those stories recount the enmity between Jacob and Esau even as they struggle in the womb of Rebekah (Gen. 25:22-23). Further conflict arises when Jacob cunningly gets Esau to sell him his birthright (Gen. 25:29-34). The conflicts come to a head when Rebekah strategizes to get Jacob to steal the deathbed blessing from Isaac (Gen. 27:1-45). Because of this last conflict, Jacob runs, seeking to escape the anger of his betrayed brother.

Our Lenten reading for today of the Genesis story of Jacob recounts a journey from Beer-sheba to Haran, in which Jacob rests at Bethel. This was apparently the site of an ancient sanctuary. Here, in a dream, he saw a ladder reaching to heaven on which angels descended and ascended. This structure probably resembled the great outdoor staircases leading to the upper stories of Palestinian houses. At the top of the ladder stood the Lord, who promised Jacob that in spite of his sin he would be protected by God's presence during his sojourn outside of Canaan. Moreover, when God so determined, he would return safely to the land of his kindred and occupy the place of the firstborn. Still the bargainer, Jacob promised to serve the Lord if God would indeed protect Jacob and provide him with food, clothing, and a safe return (vv. 20-22).

The Scriptures give an honest portrait of Jacob as a deceiver who thought he could succeed through trickery and human calculation. In the context of the social structures of his time his aim was high: to receive the blessing of the firstborn, which was not a mere expression of goodwill and hope but a substantive gift which, once given, could not be taken back. For Jacob it involved not only the inheritance of Canaan but also the promise given to Abraham and Isaac of salvation for his people. The paradox of Jacob's life was that his schemes and efforts appeared to be effective: He did receive the blessing of the firstborn; his hard work and scheming in Laban's household did win him prosperity; and, most decisively, his apparent victory over God at Peniel resulted in God's blessing and the symbolic change of his name to Israel. Yet, by the end of his life, he had learned the truth of his earlier confession, "Surely, the LORD is in this place—and I did not know it!" (28:16).

The message of this story is that God chose to use a trickster and supplanter to advance the divine plan. This is apparently the paradoxical way God operates. People may mean their acts for evil, but God can use them for good: the envy of Joseph's brothers, Queen Esther's strategic placement, Abraham's willingness to sacrifice his son, the death of Jesus on the cross—all attest to God's paradoxical ways. Some acts defy logic, yet God seems to use persons in the divine plan. One may do the right thing for the wrong reason, but even that can be used for the purposes of God.

In wrestling with God, Jacob is told that he has been chosen to bring blessing. He has been promised vast lands and offspring beyond measure. The God of Abraham and Isaac promises to be Jacob's God as well and to see that he has a safe return to his own land. God is revealed to Jacob in the dream as Immanuel (v. 15).

As with Jacob, so shall it be with us. When we earnestly struggle, we are rewarded with a blessing. When we wrestle with the great doctrines of the Christian faith, we are granted wisdom and understanding. We are drawn closer to God because we have had glimpses of God's greatness. All believers are challenged to wrestle with the demons of doubt, selfishness, indecisiveness and meaninglessness. In the same way, only through the struggle can we hope to learn and to emerge victoriously.

Jacob is in awe of what has been revealed in his dream (v. 7). He understands that he may run from his father and brother but not from "the Hound of Heaven." God finds one no matter where one may be and the only appropriate response is reverence and a response of obedience.

SECOND LESSON: ROMANS 5:1-11

(For Rom. 8:31-39, see First Sunday of Lent)

Paul, in Romans 5, teaches the happy fruits of justification by faith. The transition from 4:25 begins with the word *therefore* (5:1), which introduces four benefits of justification by faith: peace, grace, hope, and love (Rom. 5:1-5).

The foundation of the detailed arguments of chapter 5 is established in vv. 1-11: When the decision of God to declare human beings not guilty becomes known to us and effective for us through our acknowledgment and grasp of that act in faith, we have *peace* with God (v. 1). Moreover, our struggle against God has reached its limit and so can go no farther, and the sovereignty of sin over us is broken. The same thing is expressed in v. 10, "we were reconciled with God," in v. 11, "we have now received reconciliation," and in v. 21, where we are told that every alien lordship has now become for us a thing of the past.

Romans 5:2 speaks about the work of Christ, which provides "access" (a word used to describe admittance into the presence of royalty) into the present blessing of *grace*, and the *hope* of glory. The hope of sharing in the glory of God relates to the glory for which human beings were created and from which they have fallen (3:23), but which they will someday experience again.

Verse 3 seems like an aside from the main argument but really makes the case that persons rejoice not just in anticipation of future glory but also in the sufferings and afflictions that produce the very hope of glory (as explained in vv. 3-5). To be sure, Christians experience a future joy of sharing in God's glory, but Paul argues that the same joy is available now, even in the midst of trials and tribulations.

In verse 4, Paul addresses the "tribulations" that first-century Christians had to endure when they refused to engage in immoral or idolatrous practices that made them countercultural and disloyal to the nation. Although the Pauline sufferings may not refer to the tribulations of ill health, sorrow, or pain, but rather to the harsh reaction of an unbelieving world, we may feel confident that when these afflictions come upon us we learn how to rely on patience, fortitude, character, hope, and God's love. Suffering is a time of testing. The *endurance* of which he speaks means an active overcoming of misfortune rather than passive acceptance. "Endurance produces *character.*" *Character* is a word used of metal that has been so heated by fire so all the impurities are refined out. The *hope* born out of suffering refers to the confidence out of suffering that God is transforming one's character, and will continue until we share in God's glory. In our present afflictions we can only glory, because they can only make us more steadfast, can only provide us with assurance, and can serve only to summon us all the more to hope (vv. 3-4).

Verse 5 presents the clearest description of how this righteous decision of God has been effected according to which the *love* of God—God's self, God's love toward us—has been poured forth into our hearts. That this has happened is the presupposition of our future salvation before the judgment of wrath (vv. 9-10). On its positive side, and in relation to the present, it is the presupposition of our hope of partaking in God's glory, of which (according to 3:23) we, as sinners, must have completely and finally fallen short. Wherever God's righteous decision has been acknowledged and grasped in faith, this has happened. Thus, God's righteous decision and the gospel that reveals it are called "God's saving power" (1:16). For this reason we glory in such hope (v. 2). It will not let us be put to shame, and the Holy Spirit is God's special gift as a fact of the new life (v. 5).

God's righteous decision has power to make peace with God for believers, to reconcile them to God, and to pour forth God's love into their hearts, because that decision has been carried out in Jesus Christ, who is uniquely (v. 7) the way by which we gain access to the grace in which we have taken our stand (v. 2). For God's love towards us commends itself in this (v. 8), that Christ died for us while we were still weak (v. 6), still sinners (v. 8), still godless (v. 6), still enemies (v. 10). God's love has, therefore, not waited for us to get right, but has come to meet us and gone before us. While one might be willing to die for a good person or a just person, no one would want to die for a wicked one—but Christ did (v. 6).

The important words *reconciled* and *reconciliation* appear in 5:10-11 for the first time in Romans. The Greek word *katallasso*, translated *reconciliation*, describes what God has done in salvation. It indicates a thorough change in relationship. Enmity is given over to friendship. God opens the way for this change in relationship, bringing harmony and peace between human beings and God.

In sovereign anticipation of our faith, God has justified us through the sacrificial blood of Christ. In the death of God's son, God has intervened on our behalf with the "nevertheless" of divine free grace in the face of the apparently insurmountable power of our revolt and resistance (vv. 9-10). So God has made peace, so reconciled us, so commended love toward us. Our future is thus tied up with the bold words "we shall be saved" (vv. 9-10), and there is nothing left to us but to glory in our existence. On the death of God's Son there follows his life as the Risen One (v. 10). When we put our faith in God's righteous decision carried out in Christ Jesus, we immediately become sharers in Christ's triumph.

The one who saves in this manner functions differently from those whom he saves. His function is giving; our function is receiving. His function is leading the way; our function is following. Romans 5:1-21 points out that in Christ the one justified by faith has peace with God. This faith is a source of hope for the future and a source of power for the present (5:1-5). The atoning act of Christ is cause for rejoicing because those who were "enemies" of God and had every right to fear the consequences of the wrath of God are now at peace and are saved by that atoning work (5:6-11). Jesus Christ has changed our human condition.

What happens to patience and character when it seems that the family is going through a breakdown? What happens to the power of patience and strength of character when children are in rebellion against everything that one stands for or has been taught about right living? What happens to patience and character and the power to endure when no job is present, bills are due, and one is on the brink of disaster? Paul responds that no matter what the problem, one is never alone. It is never just me and my problems, for God's love is always with us. The Holy Spirit fills our hearts with God's love (v. 5). This is the first time the Holy Spirit is evoked in Romans, but it will emerge as the power that helps us to appropriate the presence of God within us and the life of Christ in our daily walking, no matter what the test.

What keeps the Christian going is the fact that God's love is present. If everyone seems to forsake and if problems seem too great to bear, the Christian is reminded that God cares, that God loves. God loves one even before one is lovable, while one is a sinner. While we were yet sinners God showed love toward us by sending Christ to die for us (v. 8). We have joy and rejoice because God has died for our sins and brought reconciliation so that we are restored in the family of God (v. 11).

God has done more for us than many are willing to do for one another. We have taken marriage vows to love our mates in sickness and in health, for richer or for poorer, and to remain faithful unto that one as long as both shall live. Yet, when sickness, poverty, or infidelity comes, our love thins out. The remarkable thing about God's love is that God loves not *because* of but *in spite* of. "While we still were sinners Christ died for us." This point is made even more emphatically in Romans 5:12-21.

The African family works on a communal basis: "I am because we are." The Western mindset is so geared to individual success that it is sometimes difficult to understand this corporate personality attitude, or that of the Jewish community. When Achan sinned, his sin affected the whole community (Josh. 7:6-26). The Jews thought in terms of tribe, nation, community. On the basis of this communitarian perspective, Paul argues that the death of Jesus saved us all as the sin of one man condemned us all. One man, Adam, brought sin, disobedience, death, punishment, and judgment upon humankind. One man, Jesus Christ, through obedience, brought mercy, grace, forgiveness, and life.

GOSPEL: MARK 8:31-38

Mark 8:31-38 appears in the context of 8:27—10:45, where Mark makes clear the nature of the call to discipleship that Jesus offers—discipleship in light of the cross of Jesus. The Gospel parallels to this section in Mark are Matthew 16:13—18:9 and in Luke 9:18—50.

Today's Gospel lesson transpires in Caesarea Philippi, a territory ruled by Philip, the brother of Herod Antipas who ruled Galilee. Because Jesus' ministry is beginning to get stormy, he desires to retreat from the territory of Herod so he can have some quiet time with the disciples.

According to the Gospels, Jesus made reference to his approaching death on four different occasions. First, at Caesarea Philippi (Mark 8:31-33; Matt. 16:21-23; Luke 9:22); second, in Galilee (Mark 9:30-32; Matt. 18:22-23; Luke 9:43-45); third, on the way to Jerusalem (Mark 10:31-34; Matt. 20:17-19; Luke 18:31-34). His last mention of his approaching death is in Jerusalem itself at the Passover meal (Mark 14:17-21; Matt. 26:20-25; Luke 22:21-23; John 13:21-30). It is interesting that all these announcements are reported in all the Synoptics. It is also interesting to note the locations where these predictions are reported to have been said.

Caesarea Philippi is the seat of the Roman power in Palestine, and the center of the Roman god. It is a Gentile and a Roman religious city located close to the snow-capped Mount Hermon, a beautiful area with rich soil. Pan, the Greek god of nature, has a temple nearby. We are not told that Jesus is in the city but that he is in the region or in its villages, as in Mark. A white temple in honor of the Roman Emperor whom the worshipers saw as a god is situated on the hillside. There Peter makes his confession about the identity of Jesus, affirming him as the Messiah (v. 29). Jesus admonishes the disciples not to tell who he is (v. 30).

In this region he asks them who people think he is and what the disciples think he is. After Peter's reply and Jesus' commendation, Jesus tells them of his coming death. This is followed by the teaching on self-denial and taking up one's cross to follow Jesus. What prompted the question about his personhood and his death? His presence here reminds him of Jerusalem, the city of God's people.

The other three places in which the confessions take place include Galilee, on the way to Jerusalem, and in Jerusalem. *Galilee* is the center of the religious sects and political revolutionary groups. *On the way to Jerusalem* is the anticipation of the reaction of the main Jewish parties (Pharisees and Sadducees) who realized the popularity Jesus had received. Not only that, the entry into Jerusalem is not a great and glorious entry like that of a king into a conquered territory; rather it is as a king on an ass. *In Jerusalem,* death is not far away and rumors of the arrest of Jesus are going around. These places and circumstances are ideal ones for capturing the question of Jesus' identity and mission.

The historical Jesus must have known that his conduct and sayings put him in danger of rejection and death. Even though this is true, most scholars imply from the form and structure of these predictions that they are literary devices which heighten the developing drama of the narrative. The drama is building to the passion and death of Jesus the Messiah.

Following the confession of Peter that Jesus is the Messiah (Mark 8:27-30), Jesus begins to tell the disciples the nature of his messiahship as Son of man (v. 31). While Jesus did not say that he was Messiah, he seemed to believe that his mission was to execute the role of Messiah under the title Son of man. Why is this?

First, Jesus associated his messiahship with the Son of man who must suffer and die. The idea of a suffering Messiah did not correspond with the dominant view of Jewish piety. The "Anointed One" was to be chosen and appointed by God. Some thought he would be an earthly king, reigning with a magnificence of luxury and power equal only to the glorious days of the earlier "Son of David," King Solomon, whose empire had extended from the Dead Sea to the Mediterranean. The reign would extend to the Gulf of Akabah and the border of Egypt.

Connected with this view of Messiah is that of a conquering hero. This view stems from the belief that the Messiah would be a descendant of King David, the warrior king. The coming Anointed One would vindicate the people of God, the Jews, over their enemies (see *Assumption of Moses* 10:8-10). The Messiah would be a nationalistic figure who would punish the enemies of the Jews. The need for such a deliverer at the birth of Jesus was seen as real among the Jewish community. The people desired a restoration of Israel in Palestine from the domination of the Romans.

Others thought he would be a purely supernatural figure coming on the clouds of heaven, the "Son of man" or the "Primal man," or "the "man from heaven," who would judge the whole world, its kings and potentates, both human beings and angels, and even the demons and all who have led the world astray. Then, after the last judgment, the Anointed One would bring into being the purely heavenly, transcendental, spiritual existence that should last throughout eternity.

"Son of man" is a much debated title both with regard to its meaning and whether it was a title Jesus attributed to himself. It originally indicated a human being as in Ezekiel (2:1) and Psalms (8:4). Used in this manner to refer to Jesus, the title expressed Jesus' solidarity with humanity as well as his role as mediator and representative of humanity before God.

The title "Son of man" appears with a different tinge in the apocalypse of Daniel where the prophet sees "one like a son of man coming on the clouds of heaven" (Dan. 7:13). This view probably derived from the failure of royal messiahs in the history of Israel. Israel had been destroyed in 722 B.C.E. by the Assyrians. This was followed by the fall of Jerusalem and exile to Babylon in 587 B.C.E. at the hand of Nebuchadnezzar. While these two events did not deter the expectation of a messiah in the lineage of David, even into New Testament times, other events caused the people of Israel to postulate some other figure. Frustration and failure of the Hasmonean leadership in which priest-kings were one and the same, coupled with the rise of the Greco-Roman occupation of a restored Judah, also precipitated an ideal figure. This was a change because the Messiah seems no longer to be a human agent like king, priest, prophet, Cyrus, or one of the Davidic line. One sees this shift clearly in later Judaism and in apocalyptic writings, such as in the Parables of Enoch, consisting of chapters 37–71 of the pseudepigraphal *Book of Enoch*. Here one of the ideal figures was the "Son of man," who became symbolic of Israel, of the "elect," and finally signified the righteous or "eschatological judge," a semi-divine individual who would appear as judge of the nations (Dan. 7:13; Matt. 26:64; Mark 14:62; Luke 22:69; Rev. 1:13).

The role of this Son of man was to destroy heaven and earth, send sinners to everlasting punishment, destroy the kingdoms of this world, and establish the righteous in a new heaven and earth where this figure would reign at God's right hand forever. This apocalyptic mindset was very strong in the time of Jesus. While some have doubted whether Jesus saw himself as the apocalyptic Son of man, there is no serious reason to doubt that Jesus used this term of himself, as representative of humanity as a whole, and as the coming "Son of man" (Mark 14:62; Luke 9:58).

In verse 32, the writer contends that all who heard understood what Jesus said, but clearly they did not. Peter "rebukes" Jesus. This word *epitiman* is used in Mark as a word of power against those forces perceived to be against the will of God (cf. 1:25-27). Peter and Jesus use the same word of rebuke. Peter seems to think that Jesus' talk about suffering goes against God's will. What kind of God would stand for a suffering Messiah or a suffering believer? In this narrative, Jesus takes Peter to task as he turns to him while addressing the disciples.

Jesus rebukes Peter. He speaks a word of power as an antidote to a force that he perceives as a test. Peter is on the side of "Satan" trying to dissuade Jesus from being faithful to the will of God. Peter wanted a Messiah in his own image. Jesus does not give in to the test. He is clearly on "the side of God and not of men." Jesus will not fit Peter's agenda because he has one of his own.

The tragedy of our day is that we still have members in churches who are following Jesus because they feel that he can make them healthy, wealthy, and wise and have forgotten that membership is not discipleship. Discipleship is costly and if there is no *cross* there is no *crown*.

Jesus was careful not to engage the disciples on false pretenses. He did not offer his disciples merely a religion that could make one healthy, wealthy, and wise. He did not conceal the sacrifices that would be required of them, the cross that would be theirs to bear, the cup that would be theirs to drink (Mark 8:34-38; 10:38-39). All would-be followers were forced to think through the implications of their decision and to recognize the cost involved before taking the plunge. Peter recoiled from the idea of the suffering of God's servant who came at the end of the age. Jesus rebukes Peter because Jesus plainly stated the idea of a suffering servant Son of man (v. 32). This is reiterated in Mark's account even after the experience at Caesarea Philippi, because the disciples did not understand the nature of his messiahship in terms of service and faithful obedience (9:31; 10:33).

"Get behind me, Satan" means simply "Don't try to change my mission with that kind of talk." The rebuke of Peter is stated against him as one who is speaking on behalf of the tempter, Satan. Already in 1:13 Satan puts Jesus to the test and tries to get him to betray his mission by being what others wanted him to be. Jesus, however, is seeking to do God's will and judges all other suggestions in the light of that objective. Jesus probably stayed away from the title "Messiah" precisely because its content had so many meanings, none of which adequately captured his mission.

Jesus was not talking about a Marxist revolution that might take the form of economic, political, or military changes. Jesus' revolution was much bigger. He wished to overthrow and defeat Satan and evil in order to bring order and peace on earth. The amazing thing for Peter and the disciples was that this change in the world order was to be accomplished through suffering and death. Jesus says to Peter: "For you are setting your mind not on divine things, but on human things" (8:33). Jesus refuses to be the kind of Messiah Peter wanted. To be on God's side is to trust God to show God's self in suffering, and accept Jesus on his terms and not purely on our own presuppositions. Jesus was God's Messiah and seems to have chosen a different title, filling it with a life of suffering service to humanity and faithful obedience to God's will. He had to die for others because truthtelling and acting in obedience to God's will entail consequences in a world that defies both.

According to Mark 8:34-38, there are conditions of discipleship. In the three prediction passages of Mark, discipleship is characterized simply as following in the footsteps of Jesus. In the first prediction, Jesus reproaches Peter for suggesting that he take steps to avoid suffering. Rather, Jesus says this is precisely what must be chosen (8:34-35). Following the second prediction (9:12f.), Jesus further specifies the conditions of discipleship (Mark 9:35) and after the third prediction (10:32-33), he adds yet more (Mark 10:43-45).

Just as Jesus has to suffer, so do his followers. In v. 34, Jesus says, "Follow me." This meant losing oneself in service to others as one sought to be obedient to God's will. "For those who want to save their life will lose it." This is true because trust in human security and selfish service does not open one up to the will of God. On the other hand, "Those who lose their life will save it" (v. 35). This verse indicates that one who gives oneself away in loving service to others and in obedience to God's will, will have the security of God. Mark was concerned about loving service to others but also he adds that one who loses one's life in loyalty to the gospel shall have the security of God.

Verses 36-37 are tied together with the same Greek word for life. One may gain everything the world has to give and yet lose the one thing that God gives, life. Real life, eternal life, and life with God now and in the future is God's gift to be received now in faith. Discipleship means knowing the triumphant Son of man will come in judgment and that he will vindicate his followers.

Third Sunday in Lent

Lutheran	Roman Catholic	Episcopal	Common Lectionary
Exod. 20:1-17	Exod. 20:1-3, 7-8, 12-17	Exod. 20:1-17	Exod. 20:1-17
1 Cor. 1:22-25	1 Cor. 1:22-25	Rom. 7:13-25	1 Cor. 1:22-25
John 2:13-22	John 2:13-25	John 2:13-22	John 2:13-22

FIRST LESSON: EXODUS 20:1-17

For a long time it has been standard practice to read the Decalogue (Exod. 20:1-17) on this Sunday in Lent. Together with the assigned Gospel reading (John 2:13-22) and the Epistle (1 Cor. 1:22-25), the setting is established for reflection upon the righteousness and holiness of God's inclusive grace and judgment.

While the commandments are given in the context of community, they themselves are addressed to individuals: "You shall not." Most of the Ten Commandments are negative in form, indicating what the people should not do. These are prohibitions with no attempt to depict particular contexts for application or penalties for violation. They are general principles that evoke the need for particular cases and contexts.

The Ten Commandments provide the foundation for ethical behavior in the Old Testament: love God; worship only God; do not abuse God's character by misusing God's name; allow rest for yourself, your family, and employees; honor parents; do not murder, commit adultery, steal, lie, or place designs on the property of others. Even though stated negatively, these moral rules are essential for meaningful community existence.

It is significant that the law was given within the context of the Sinai Covenant. According to the account in Exodus, God called Moses to Mount Sinai, and prior to giving the Ten Commandments, offered to covenant with the people to continue as their God and make them a holy nation among the nations (Exod. 19:4-6).

At Mount Sinai, God established a covenant community, then provided rules for community living. The Ten Commandments were not "nice to have"; they were essential norms for transforming a group of escaped slaves into a community that could survive in the wilderness and gain a promised land. Community was not possible without honesty, trust, the keeping of promises, and respect for life, family, and property.

The Ten Commandments are part of the Sinai covenant made with the whole people of Israel. For Israel, the covenant with God meant freedom and obligations for the individual and community. Those who have had the experience of being delivered, have an obligation to live as exodus people.

The first three commandments define our relationship with God (20:1-7). We are addressed with dignity and called to a response that acknowledges God's powerful presence in our midst. Thus, exodus people have an undivided loyalty to God who brings freedom. Exodus people do not attempt to manipulate God by carving or worshiping empty idols. Exodus people do not take the power of the Lord's name lightly, swearing oaths they do not mean.

First Commandment: "You shall have no other gods before me." This is the first and central commandment of Israel. The world in which the ancient Hebrews lived evidently exercised belief in other gods. This command prohibits the worship of other deities in conjunction with Yahweh. While no denial is made of the existence of other gods, there is a definite prohibition of amalgamating other gods with Yahweh.

Second Commandment: "You shall not make for yourself a graven image." This commandment prohibits the making and worship of images and likenesses of foreign gods or even of Yahweh in Israel's worship. The emphasis seems to have been on the latter. Yahweh communicated God's self in word and action and not primarily through images by which persons could exercise control over the power of God.

Third Commandment: "You shall not take the name of the LORD your God in vain." One should not use Yahweh's name to support a false oath (Lev. 19:12). One should not use the divine name to manipulate the divine power and presence. To avoid taking the name of God in vain is to take positively the name of God in earnest by living in a way that is consistent with God's holy will and purpose.

The other commandments turn to mutual, caring, human relationships (20:8-17).

The Fourth Commandment: "Remember the sabbath day, and keep it holy." This and the following commandment are positive statements. The seventh day is one without work. Since Yahweh rested on the seventh day in the creation of the world, that seventh day is made holy and thus blessed. The work and rest pattern is the one God ordained for Israel and the followers of Yahweh. Sabbath is a day for recognition that our time is not our own but is God-given; that the whole of creation is God-given; that the sabbath is a cathedral in time in which the praise of God is supreme. Exodus people honor a day of rest, reminded of the contrast between oppressive work and a time for recreation.

The Fifth Commandment: "Honor your father and your mother, so that your days may be long in the land that the LORD your God is giving you." "Honor" probably means to submit to the authority of, to pay respect, care for, and recognize the dignity of one's parents. The long life is intended for Israel and the longevity of the clan rather than initially to the individual. Even though respect given to the adult parent may enrich one's life, this promise is no magic wand that needs to be waved to extend one's life on earth. Exodus people honor their parents, remembering that family relationships provide the foundation for community.

This extends also to the idea of respecting and listening to the elders. They have the responsibility of passing on the faith and positive values. In the black church tradition, the "Mother of the Church" is one who is highly respected for her deep faith, deep conviction, and tremendous overcoming of life's troubles. The same is true of the "Father of the Church," who is often characterized as a "pillar." There is a sense in which the tradition resides in the elders who embrace the extended family, especially the extended family or household of God.

The Sixth Commandment: "You shall not murder." This command does not have an object and thus invites speculation as to whom one should refrain from killing. Most would contend that the object is a human being. It does not refer probably to killing in war or the death penalty, but to murder or killing not authorized by the community or courts. In Israel's history it was probably given as a command to avoid killing out of vengeance taken by a goel or avenger for the death of a clan or family member. Such a prohibition recognizes and appreciates the value of human life and peace within the context of community living.

The Seventh Commandment: "You shall not commit adultery." This command does not have an object either. The general consensus is that the object is understood to be the wife or betrothed woman of another man in the Israelite community. Adultery is a threat to paternity and the stability of the family. Since the name of the father's household had to be propagated, nothing that threatened this should be tolerated. While this injunction may have ethical implications, the command concerning adultery did not deal specifically with sexual ethics. The man committed adultery against another Israelite man while the woman committed adultery against her marriage. In either case, both had to suffer the penalty of death (Deut. 22:22, Lev. 20:10).

The Eighth Commandment: "You shall not steal." The object also is not given in this case, consistent with the sixth and seventh commandments. The general meaning of *steal* is to take or misappropriate either things or persons. Some have contended that the meaning is to steal a human being or to sell another into slavery. This corresponds with Exodus 21:16, which prohibits kidnapping. We should not neglect to see, however, that the command not to steal also must refer to property. To steal one's property is an attack on the labor of others and the blessings that God has given to others. Human rights and property rights need to be protected from the theft of others. This is the loving responsibility of a community (Lev. 19:11). Exodus people do not kill, violate the marriages of others, or steal, for life is too precious to be abused or perverted.

The Ninth Commandment: "You shall not bear false witness against your neighbor." The evidence points toward this commandment being one that prohibits false witness in a court system (Exod. 23:2; Deut. 19:16-19; Prov. 14:5), even though this command has been taken as a general prohibition against lying. Of course, to be a good witness in courts presupposes that one speaks the truth in everyday life. Exodus people do not give false testimony in the administration of justice.

The Tenth Commandment: "You shall not covet." This command seems to put emphasis on the inner attitude of a person. Some interpreters have tried to connect the Hebrew Scriptures' meaning of *covet* with the taking of action to obtain that which one covets. However, the general consensus is that *covet* is mainly about an inner impulse or craving (Prov. 13:4; 2 Sam. 23:15; Num. 11:4). After affirming the basic meaning of covet as an inner attitude, one still recognizes that the story of every sin is summarized as first the thought, then the form, fascination with the form, and then the fall. In reality, coveting and making plans to take go hand in hand. A change of heart leads to a change of behavior, as the tenth commandment shows. Exodus people do not covet, for they have learned under the tyranny of a Pharaoh how oppressive greed can be.

These normative principles, established in the Sinai covenant, were continued in the proclamations of the eighth-century prophets and reinforced with a strong injunction against oppression and injustice. In strong language, Amos roars God's disapproval because the Israelites ignored his commandments: "I hate, I despise your festivals. . . . Let justice roll down like waters, and righteousness like an everflowing stream" (Amos 5:21, 24).

Jesus emphasized the importance of God's commandments: "Do not think that I have come to abolish the law or the prophets; I have not come to abolish but to fulfill" (Matt. 5:17). What he did seek to abolish with the "new law" (Matthew 5–7) was hypocrisy and legalism. He emphasized that moral rules should form internal attitudes and motives as well as external actions. He called for integrity and genuineness. He counseled to refrain from acts of murder, adultery, and lying, but, more profoundly, to avoid attitudes of hate, lust, and deceitfulness. Jesus viewed the law as ethical principles and guides, not legalistic rules and empty ritual.

So we now must learn to live in a community that by its very presence is meant to exemplify to the world an alternative style of life. The boundaries that are placed on our freedom are boundaries that separate us from the chaos of anarchy. Our self-centeredness and alienation from others is the path that leads to death and slavery. At the same time, only by allowing individuals their own dignity and responsibility can our collective community fulfill the calling to become a holy people.

SECOND LESSON: 1 CORINTHIANS 1:22-25

In 1 Corinthians 1:22-25, we encounter one of Paul's paradoxical statements regarding the truth of the Gospel: The folly of the cross is wisdom. This insight is in the context of 1 Corinthians 1–4 where Paul is concerned about divisions in the church. These divisions have occurred because the Corinthians have a wrong conception of wisdom, the community, and of the Christian ministry. Paul thinks that those causing divisions in the body have misunderstood the character of the Gospel.

The words *wisdom* and *wise* are used twenty-six times in chapters 1–3, and only eighteen more times in all of Paul's letters. Evidently, the audience to whom Paul is addressing this letter was steeped in a wisdom derived from itinerant philosophers who were plentiful in the Greek world of Paul's day. The text itself does not tell us what this wisdom was, but we can assume that the Corinthian Christians were beginning to think of their new Christian faith as a new divine wisdom. This manner of looking at the faith also caused them to evaluate their leaders in human terms as they might any of the itinerant philosophers.

If the Corinthian Christians would have evaluated Paul on the basis of the stylish, brilliant, clever, and entertaining traveling Greek philosophers, he would not have compared well. We are told Paul was not a brilliant speaker. For example, he could not compare with the silver-tongued Apollos (1:12; 3:4; 4:6), as he readily admitted. He did not have a charming personality. He earned his living as a tentmaker, and did not have a stylish appearance. Furthermore, that which Paul preached called for a strict and rigid discipline. Such preaching would not have much appeal to some people in the Corinthian church who thought that the Christian faith revolved around a privileged knowledge (Greek: *gnosis*). Such thinking would make questions of ethics of strictly secondary importance. Paul had to argue on the basis of the wisdom of God as compared with the wisdom of human beings. He determined to preach just one message, Jesus Christ, and him crucified (1 Cor. 2:2—3:10).

Paul asserts that the foolish dying of the human Jesus on the cross revealed the wisdom of God. The cross is indeed the very wisdom of God. At the point of weakness and brokenness of Christ, God acts to show God's power and wisdom. Paul believed that this is the way God acts. All things, including miracles, knowledge, wisdom, power, the pride of race, high birth, and the established order of things, are subordinate to the one nailed to a cross, whose folly is wisdom. This is indeed a paradox.

God has abandoned the wisdom of this world (1:18-22, 27-28; 3:18-20). At the heart of the Christian gospel is the word of the cross (1:18-25), foolishness to the Greeks, and a scandal to the Jews. It is foolishness to the Greeks because it does not appear to have intellectual explanation. It is a scandal to the Jews because the cross signifies for them defeat and shame. It is the reverse of their long-expected and triumphant Messiah, setting up a glorious earthly kingdom here and now. Paul's answer is that Christ, through the cross, has "become for us wisdom from God" (1:30) and this wisdom is revealed by the Spirit to those who have the Spirit.

The mystery of God's action throughout history has been how God takes the fragile nature of the words and actions of ordinary people to convey the truth and salvation of God's self. Paul summarizes the mystery of God well: God "chose what is weak in the world to shame the strong" (1 Cor. 1:27).

ALTERNATE SECOND LESSON: ROMANS 7:13-25

Romans 7:13-25 is a very complex passage. If these words are concerned with Paul's own experience, these questions are raised: (1) When he tells of inner warfare, is he speaking of former days in his life before he trusted Jesus Christ for salvation? Or (2) is he sharing out of his Christian journey following salvation but prior to sanctification (receiving the fullness of the life of faith)? Augustine originally applied the passage to the unconverted, but later came to insist that Paul had in mind the converted Christian. This latter Augustinian view was taken up by Martin Luther and heightened almost to the point of a dogma. A typical comment of Luther runs: "[In verse 14 we have] proof of a spiritual and wise man. He knows that he is carnal, and he is displeased with himself . . . but the proof of a foolish, carnal man is this, that he regards himself as spiritual and is pleased with himself."

Recent exegetes have tended to see 7:13-25 as Paul's autobiographical depiction of a man under the law and apart from the grace of God. The other view is the Augustinian/Lutheran view. But there are serious problems with either view when rigidly argued. C. L. Mitton has offered a mediating view: Romans 7:13-25 is depicting every person's struggle to do what is righteous through one's own efforts, apart from God's grace and Spirit. In its autobiographical format, Paul looks back and sees clearly from his new perspective of faith just how futile were those days as a rabbi seeking to storm his way to heaven by self-help. But it is equally applicable to every Christian. Experience has taught that it is ever so easy to slip from grace to prideful legalism. It threatened Paul's church at Galatia. It may well have been threatening Rome. It still happens whenever grace gives way to legalism, and one starts out on one's own holy pilgrimage to righteousness. (See for various arguments pro and con, C. Leslie Mitton, "Romans VII Reconsidered," *Expository Times* 65: 78–81, 99–103, 132–35).

The latter interpretation is very well suited to the context. In 6:1—7:6 Paul discussed the new basis for righteous life through death of the old person and incorporation into the new. Romans 7:7-25 is no digression. Paul does not suddenly return to a discussion of the inadequacy of the law to save (chaps. 1–3). On the contrary, he now turns to a final discussion of the law out of a consideration of which the Judaizing movement has made him painfully aware: The law is also an inadequate basis for the moral righteousness of the believer. Thus, he never says what popular Christianity has often taught: that after one experiences Christ, then one can fulfill the law. For Paul, the way of the law can never be the basis for Christian morality, because it always involves self-endeavor. Even Christian morality must derive from grace, from the Spirit of God.

The main theme of 7:13-25 is thus the futility of human effort to attain true righteousness. Karl Barth consistently interprets the "I" of this passage as "religious man" and the law as "religion." Religion, seen as human effort to reach God, is indeed epitomized in "law." It is the noblest of all human effort, but it is still human effort, and in the end inevitably "shatters on God."

Paul begins with a question from an imaginary objector: "Did the good law cause death?" "Certainly not," says Paul, "sin caused death" (7:13; cf. 6:23). But the law served to reveal the presence of sin, to bring out its true colors (7:7). At verse 14, Paul switches to the present tense, an important observation for the "converted Christian" interpretation of this passage. This is probably no more than a device of dramatic heightening, however. The real significance of this verse is in setting forth the basic dualistic thesis that runs throughout the passage—the spiritual versus the carnal. The law represents God's holy will, and thus is good and spiritual. The "fly in the ointment" is the human self, the old self-striving ego (7:14). It is the carnal. Paul never calls the human, physical nature evil in itself. Rather, it constitutes the vulnerable part of a person that sin so easily, so inevitably, seizes (v. 14).

Verses 15-17 depict this basic breach in the will of the person who seeks to follow the law. One knows what is right and is in basic agreement with the goodness of the law (7:16). One wills what is right (7:18), but does what is hateful to one's will (7:15). The law reveals to human beings what God wants from them but the law gives them no power to execute. Left to one's own motives, one falls under the power of sin. One's actions directly contradict one's best intentions.

How can this be? Verse 18 provides the answer. Human nature (flesh) has no independent power of its own. It becomes the "dwelling place"— "sin's host"—of powerful forces from without. Again, Paul has in mind the idea of two power spheres. A person in the *flesh* is a person apart from God. Such a person is left to oneself, and a person left to oneself inevitably falls under the power of sin. But the law enlightens one's "inner self" (v. 22), makes one yearn for the good that sin ever thwarts, and creates this unbearable moral tension between a will for the good and an actual deportment that is already captive to the power of sin (v. 23).

For such a "religious man or woman" the only remaining possibility seems a cry of despair: "I, wretch that I am, who will deliver me from this death-bound body so sold to sin?" (v. 24). Is this rhetorical question expecting no answer? No, a triumphal rejoinder seems to be on the way in verse 25a: "Thanks be to God through Jesus Christ our Lord." Thanks for what? The answer is clearly in the text, but not until chapter 8. Thank God that in divine grace human beings are justified in Christ Jesus, no longer standing under the condemning sentence (8:1). Thank God that we don't have to rely on the futility of our own powers in striving to live holy lives. We are free in Christ from the power of sin (8:2). We now have the power of the indwelling Spirit for a righteous life (8:4). This is all on the basis of faith.

GOSPEL: JOHN 2:13-22

The author of John tells the reader something about himself and his purposes in what is emphasized in 20:30-31. He wants to convince others to make a faith commitment: "Now Jesus did many other signs in the presence of his disciples, which are not written in this book. But these are written that you may come to believe that Jesus is the Messiah, the Son of God, and that through believing you may have life in his name." He thus has a point of view that he wishes his readers also to accept. He is not interested in merely pursuing the historical facts for their own sake. He wants to propagate the historic significance of Jesus so that a decision about him can be made by the readers. The cleansing of the temple fits well into that purpose.

All of the other Gospels have accounts of the cleansing of the temple. Their accounts are remarkably similar: Jesus is in Jerusalem during a feast period, he enters the temple precincts, he drives out those who were selling animals used for the temple sacrifices as well as those who were changing money, he tips over the tables of those engaging in these activities, and he defends his activity by a saying referring to "my father's house," accusing the temple audience of somehow corrupting the appropriate use of the temple. In all the accounts, shortly after the cleansing, the Jewish authorities ask Jesus by what authority he does these things.

The setting of John's temple cleansing is at Passover, the time of remembrance of the exodus. It was in the exodus that Israel was confronted with the demands of a holy and righteous God. In like manner, Israel must face a holy God in their desecration of the temple. What is the act that incurs the wrath of Jesus? It is not his frustration with those who had antagonized him for all his ministry (as might have been the case in the Synoptics). After all, only two chapters have been read about Jesus and they indicate that Jesus is popular, having just performed the sign of turning water to wine.

It seems that the temple functionaries, especially money changers, were performing a needed service. Roman coins, which were used in Jerusalem for commerce, had to be changed to shekels to pay temple tax. Even if the temple sacrifices in the form of an unspotted ox, sheep, or pigeon were to be offered to God, as required by Scripture, one needed to purchase them from temple merchants. The money changers were doing a necessary chore. The problem was that they had made the temple service a transaction rather than a meeting place for the holy and righteous God. For many it was a place where functionary arrangements were made. There was fraud in the exchanging of money. The temple treasury only accepted money coined by the temple administrators, since pagan coins with pagan images were unacceptable. Yet, the fair rate of exchange was never given.

The animals sacrificed to God were to be without blemish. A system had developed, however, in which a worshiper seldom brought an acceptable animal, and had to buy another from the priest-controlled system at an unreasonable price. Fraud had no doubt developed in the temple.

The presence of the money changers in the court of the Gentiles, the area set aside for devout Gentiles to come and pray to the true God, and the marketlike atmosphere must have detracted from the worshiplike atmosphere God intended for the temple. Furthermore, by taking the area away from the Gentiles, with no realization of their witness, the Jews had taken away this area and desecrated it. This angered Jesus.

"God, I go to church and pay my tithes, sing, pray, read scripture, and listen to a sermon because I want you to make me healthy, wealthy, and wise." At Lent we stand before a holy God, whose ways are not our ways and who is provoked to indignation by an attitude that asks, "What's in it for me?"

There are extensive differences in the Gospel accounts. Unlike the Synoptic Gospels, John has situated Jesus' cleansing of the temple at the beginning of his ministry rather than as a precipitating event leading to his death. As suggested by scholars, the final editor of John quite possibly may have moved the cleansing in John from the prepassion narrative of the Synoptics for editorial and/or theological reasons. At the very beginning of Jesus' ministry is a conflict between Jesus and establishment values that lead to his death on the cross. One is not surprised by the typical irony in John. When Jesus speaks of "this temple," his audience thinks he is talking about the Herodian temple that took forty-six years to build. The reader, however, knowing the end of the story, knows that Jesus is speaking metaphorically and figuratively of his own body. Jesus' antagonists in John may destroy his body because of their anger against his assault on their values, but the resurrection will make him victorious.

At the very beginning of the Gospel, Jesus comes with braided whip. He overturns the tables as in the Synoptics but merely orders the pigeon sellers out instead of overturning their seats. The author seems to confront the reader at the beginning with a righteous God who demands not transactions but true worship. True worship does not seek what we can get if we obey the Ten Commandments, or entice God to bless us by our own standards of blessing. After all 1 Corinthians 1:22-25 reminds us that God overturns our own expectations and chooses those whom the world accounts as unwise to be the recipients of God's unfathomable grace. Jesus was insisting that the Jews examine their sense of purpose and worship that they seemed to have forgotten. The temple was the Father's house and not that of the Jews.

Fourth Sunday in Lent

Lutheran	Roman Catholic	Episcopal	Common Lectionary
Num. 21:4-9	2 Chron. 36:14-16, 19-23	2 Chron. 36:14-23	2 Chron. 36:14-23
Eph. 2:4-10	Eph. 2:4-10	Eph. 2:4-10	Eph. 2:4-10
John 3:14-21	John 3:14-21	John 6:4-15	John 3:14-21

FIRST LESSON: NUMBERS 21:4-9

In the book of Numbers, we encounter a band of escaped slaves who are murmuring and complaining about their condition in the wilderness. They had been released by God from slavery and oppression in Egypt. Yet, they are uncomfortable because they had been taken from the familiar to the unfamiliar. They no longer can count on the daily routine of work and the security of someone else providing for their livelihood. They now have to depend upon the provision of God for food, which they received in the form of manna (Exod. 16:12, 31-35), quail (Exod. 16:12-13), and water (Exod. 15:22-25). They preferred Egypt to the uncertainty of the wilderness. They wanted freedom but not the responsibility or consequences of freedom.

In our text for today, the people are reminded that God had provided for their needs and yet they complain against the leadership of Moses. Nor do they like God's food policy. Hope is dying in the providential powers of God. Evidently, this passage is written by someone who had the belief that if one suffered it was because of an evil deed that one had done. The remedy for those suffering from the bite of poisonous snakes is for Moses to lift a poisonous serpent of bronze on a pole. Those who look at it are healed.

There is a saying that makes the point that success is getting what one wants, but happiness is wanting what one gets. This is always the dilemma of life. Ambition and ability can lead persons to accomplishments, but only those committed and faithful to the will of God can be truly happy.

ALTERNATE FIRST LESSON: 2 CHRONICLES 36:14-23

This reading forms a link between the reading from Exodus on the Third Sunday, and that from Jeremiah which follows on the Fifth Sunday.

It tells of the rupture of the Sinai Covenant, of the infidelity of Israel, and of the consequences of the national betrayal of Yahweh at all levels: "All the leading priests and the people also were exceedingly unfaithful, following all the abominations of the nations. . . . But they kept mocking the messengers of God, despising his words, and scoffing at his prophets, until the wrath of the Lord against his people became so great that there was no remedy" (2 Chron. 36:14, 16).

Again, Israel's fate is the responsibility of the entire community. There is no one scapegoat to blame for the trials and tribulations of the nation: All have sinned and reneged on the covenant. The people have not listened to the prophets and the rulers have strayed from God's guidance; now they must suffer the consequences of their actions.

First and Second Chronicles are not scriptural books from which ministers usually preach; a brief background is therefore in order. Traditionally, 1 and 2 Chronicles, Ezra, and Nehemiah have been attributed to the same author. Today, however, some scholars feel that Ezra and Nehemiah stem from different authors. The Chronicler, whose sources were Deuteronomy through 2 Kings and the Pentateuch (the first five books of the Hebrew Scriptures), wrote an alternative theological version of Israel's history from creation to the Babylonian exile. He selectively used his sources to emphasize God's action with God's people in terms of sin and punishment, grace and renewal, faithlessness of God's people and the faithfulness of God to the covenant.

The Chronicler used his sources so freely that we can say history is made to serve the theological concerns of the author. First and Second Chronicles exercised a certain freedom in building upon the traditions that were received. Although the Chronicler is now recognized to have used various sources more carefully than was admitted by a former generation of scholars, these sources are interpreted and handled from a particular point of view and for particular purposes, as any introduction to Hebrew Scriptures will show.

For example, the verses for today's reading in 2 Chronicles 36:14-23 recount events from the reign of Zedekiah, which began after the fall of Jerusalem in 597 B.C.E., through the destruction of the city in 587 B.C.E., through the entire Babylonian exile, and to the edict of Cyrus in 538, which permitted the exiles to return home. He recounts this history by abridging and, in some cases, reinterpreting the information from his sources in 2 Kings 23–25. For example, the Chronicler states that all who were not killed were taken into exile, leaving the land without inhabitants. However, 2 Kings reports that the poorest people were left, along with Gedaliah. Some traditions found in Jeremiah 37–39 also influence the Chronicler.

Significant for the interpretation of this passage is the view, prevalent among the prophets before the fall of Jerusalem, that the exile was punishment derived from sin. This was a Deuteronomic principle that agreed essentially with 2 Kings but was later debated by the wisdom tradition of Job and others. The Chronicler, however, agrees with the principle applied to exiled Judah that one must reap what one sows. The Chronicler lists the nature of the sin and the sinners differently from 2 Kings. Second Kings blames the kings for the sin leading to the fall of Jerusalem, but the Chronicler contends that it was a punishment of the pre-exilic priests and the people who ignored the warnings of the pre-exilic prophets (v. 14).

The writer shows his priestly rewriting of Israel's history in verse 14 where he stresses that sin is unfaithfulness to God and "following all the abominations of the nations," a direct violation of the first two commandments. This means that through this unfaithfulness the temple is polluted and profaned.

In verse 16, the Chronicler squeezes the burning of the temple and destruction of Jerusalem into a single verse, and interprets the seventy years exile as a sabbath for the land of Judah, during which it lay desolate. The release of the exiles is for the rebuilding of the temple to the glory of God.

The last three verses (2 Chron. 36:20-23), a verbatim retelling of Ezra 1:1-3 that reiterates the good news of freedom, is believed added by a later editor. It was added probably because 2 Chronicles was the last book of the Hebrew canon. The editor did not want the canon to end on a note of desolation of the land but on the good news of God's deliverance.

Jerusalem and the temple are destroyed by the Babylonians, who then take the inhabitants into exile in Babylon where they remain for about seventy years in fulfillment of the prophecy of Jeremiah. During Lent, the lesson from Chronicles is that just as the Jewish community was in exile in Babylon but later returned, so the Christian is reminded that the Christian faith goes through crucifixion on to resurrection.

SECOND LESSON: EPHESIANS 2:4-10

Since Ephesians is a theological treatise rather than an epistle, its structure is not difficult to determine. Like the Colossian letter, Ephesians contains two main divisions: the first is primarily concerned with theology (1:1—3:21), while the second deals with the various applications of Christianity to specific life situations (4:1—6:24).

Our lectionary reading today is Ephesians 2:4-10, which falls in the theological division of the letter. The message of Ephesians is one of reconciliation and unity, particularly church unity in the context of world and cosmic unity. The treatise recognizes the seemingly endless conflict between good and evil (6:12), between God and rebellious human beings (2:1-2), within the church (4:1-6), and within individuals (2:3). Given this background, the author contends that God's purpose is unity, that Christ is God's agent of reconciliation, that the church is Christ's instrument of reconciliation, and unity within the church is basic to all other unity.

Whether written by Paul or one of his followers, this letter seeks to show the revelation of the mystery of God as seen in the reconciliation of Jew and Gentile. From the very beginning of the letter (1:3) to the end (6:24), there is reference to the realm of heaven. What happens in heaven has repercussions on earth (2:6). The exalted Christ who dwells in the presence of divinity is carrying out God's divine purpose: reconciliation and peace. This reconciliation and peace is not so much future as it is a present reality and a vision of hope (1:17-19). Through the imagery of baptism (Eph. 5:26), the writer makes penetrating and hope-filled observations about the Christian life.

The whole section of Ephesians 2:1-10 is to be placed alongside other summarizing passages of Pauline theology (Rom. 3:21-31; 5:1-11; 1 Cor. 1:18-25; 2 Cor. 5:16-21; and Gal. 2:14-21). Ephesians 2:4-10 stresses God's love as shown in the work of Christ on behalf of individuals. The passage 2:11-22 focuses on the church. It is true that the church is in view even when the individual is discussed and vice versa; yet 2:1-10 in a special sense focuses on the individual. We should never forget that God's righteousness entails both wrath and love. The writer of Ephesians depicts both Jew and Gentile as persons consigned to the wrath of God (2:3).

The writer of Ephesians rehearses the saving acts of God through Christ (1:3-5, 6-7, 8-10, and 11-14). In these verses respectively, Ephesians share in the privilege of being children of God, they are recipients of the grace of God that brought forgiveness, witnesses of a unified creation through Christ, and believers of the gospel acting as children of God, receiving their inheritance as children now and fully in the final glory of God.

As a result of these saving acts of God through Christ, men and women live in a new spiritual situation. This affirmation is close to the thought expressed in Colossians 1:13-20 and 2:20. Once the Ephesians were worldly and lived under the jurisdiction of evil powers. They were therefore in a state of death, but through Christ they have been made alive (2:1-3).

God, being merciful, raised men and women, even though they lived in a condition of sin, to a heavenly existence through Christ (2:4-6). The passage Ephesians 2:4-6 resembles the baptismal hymns of Paul in Romans 6 and Colossians 2:12. In Romans 6 the believer has died with Christ and lives in expectation of rising in the eschatological future. This served as a challenge to ethical living now. Colossians states that through baptism, the believer experiences death and resurrection. Ephesians 2:4-6, however, contends that through baptism the believer experiences death and resurrection with Christ and translation to heaven with Christ. This seems very gnostic in orientation, stressing that the material existence is less desirable or real than the spiritual realm. A neglect of the physical existence is rectified by what is stated in Ephesians 2:8-10.

Ephesians 2:8-10 is often given as a brief statement of Pauline theology in the New Testament. This is true even if most scholars do not believe that Paul wrote the book of Ephesians. Women and men are saved through faith by grace (2:8), which is the result not of their actions, but of God's free gift (2:7-9). All human beings are made by God, and then made complete in Christ. Good conduct on the part of human beings is the results of their relationship to Christ (2:10). Yes, we may be saved by grace through faith, but also one must live a life of faith and service. There is an indicative and imperative involved in the new creation. The indicative conveys the message that one has been saved by God's grace and appropriated by faith. The imperative contends that one must live a justified life.

The amazing announcement is that God's love and mercy constantly appears beyond the wrath. Those without hope and God now have God's love, which has been experienced and has brought life to all through Christ's mediating death. Yet, the writer looks beyond Christ's role through crucifixion and gives a preview of Christ in the heavens. Through the image of baptism, the Christ who was crucified and raised up also raises up the believer and gives the believer a place in the heavens. Through baptism the Christian is in Christ, experiences the life that comes from the mediating work of Christ, and has an eternal inheritance even when facing the power of death. God's love is indeed stronger than death.

GOSPEL: JOHN 3:14-21

In John 3–4, Jesus is concerned with representatives of Jewish tradition and untraditional persons—Nicodemus and the Samaritan woman, respectively. Nicodemus, a Pharisee and ruler of Jews, shows himself incapable of understanding and accepting God's new revelation of Jesus. He misunderstands Jesus repeatedly, because he takes his words in a literal, ordinary sense, whereas they are understood properly with reference to Jesus and his revelation. "Rebirth" is the regeneration that occurs through faith in Jesus. Similarly, in conversation with the woman of Samaria, the "living water" of which Jesus speaks is not "running water" but the water of eternal life that only Jesus can give. More than Nicodemus she is able to comprehend Jesus' words and the result of her conversation with Jesus is the conversion of a number of her compatriots (4:39-42). While Nicodemus's meeting with Jesus had no immediate positive outcome, Nicodemus himself reappears later in the Gospel to defend Jesus (7:50-52) and assist in his burial (19:39). The judgment on him is not finally negative. The fact that Nicodemus, in spite of his membership on the Jewish Supreme Court and his knowledge of the law, needs to accept the truth of needing to be born anew, leads to a discussion of what is really needed to know the truth.

In the first unit of our Gospel reading for today, John 2:14-15 compares the event of Jesus' redemptive death on the cross with Moses' lifting of the serpent on the pole in Numbers 21:4-9. Verse 14 is the first Johannine passion prediction: The Son of man must be "lifted up." As usual, John has a double meaning: The "lifting up" refers to the crucifixion and exaltation of Jesus as he returns to God (John 8:28; 12:32). In John's Gospel the meaning is the literal lifting of Jesus' body on a cross. This crucifixion was to be the crowning event of his earthly ministry so that glorification could occur.

In the Numbers story, the people considered themselves suffering God's punishment for sin, yet the lifting of a bronze serpent upon a pole provided relief and life to all who looked upon it. In like manner, Christ is lifted up and glorified for the life of all believers. John 2:14-15 and Numbers 21:4-9 bespeak the grace of God upon God's people in need of love and salvation.

The second unit, verses 16-21, is a theological interpretation of the purpose of Jesus' advent into the world. John 3:16 has been considered by many as a watershed for the Gospel of John. Verse 16 stresses the role of God in the life of Jesus. God sent Jesus into the "world." *World* is one of John's favorite words. In this context "God so loved the 'world' " means the human family that lives in this world, for whose salvation the Son was sent (3:17). Verses 16 and 17 stress two features of God's activity. God so loved Jesus, God's only child, who brings eternal life to believers (v. 16) and salvation for the world (v. 17). Jesus' presence evokes a decision. In fact, condemnation is upon anyone who refuses to trust or exercise faith in Jesus (v. 18).

Verses 19-21 use the metaphor of light and night to express realities about God's revelation. God's coming into the world in Jesus Christ is symbolized as light, and one who refuses to accept the revelation of God is considered to be in a place where there is the absence of light. Christ's coming as light brought not only eternal life but also condemnation (v. 19) of those who are evil and who prefer the night rather than the day or the light (v. 20). In 3:21, followers of Jesus are called to "do the truth." Knowledge of the truth is not sufficient. Truth is a way of acting and living. This means that truth is exemplified in Jesus' own behavior, which made the love of God real to people.

People then as now prefer to remain blind to the truth. To know is to do. People would rather kill truthtellers than seek to hear and obey their message. This is especially true when one takes sides with hurt people—one cannot do this without getting hurt. Many times the ones whom one wishes to help do not always appreciate the truthtellers' purpose. At the same time, the one whose status quo will be upset does not wish to change or hear the truth. Consequently, the truthteller will usually be in a very vulnerable place in which a cross is virtually assured.

In spite of danger, we are challenged by Jesus to take up that cross and follow him. The Christian faith is powerful precisely at this point. We are not asked to forge new paths; rather, we are urged to follow Christ who has already cut the path! Our responsibility is to carry on, continue the work already begun at creation and embodied in the life, ministry, death, and resurrection of Jesus. Jesus stated that through the Holy Spirit, we will do greater things than he did. Only by fully giving our lives to God can we, in fact, be what we were created to be—beings in the likeness and image of God. During Lent, we pause to reconsider our mission and commitment as we renew our faith.

This passage is also a great advertisement for multicultural and inter-religious unity. God's love is global and universal. We are challenged to listen and attend to our sisters and brothers and to the earth and environment. Because we recognize that we are in relationship to both, we are moved to become active in ushering in God's reign.

Fifth Sunday In Lent

Lutheran	Roman Catholic	Episcopal	Common Lectionary
Jer. 31:31-34	Jer. 31:31-34	Jer. 31:31-34	Jer. 31:31-34
Heb. 5:7-9	Heb. 5:7-9	Heb. 5:5-10	Heb. 5:7-10
John 12:20-33	John 12:20-33	John 12:20-33	John 12:20-33

FIRST LESSON: JEREMIAH 31:31-34

This is the last Sunday in Lent and the first day of Holy Week. The first lesson refers to the new covenant spoken of by Jeremiah. Jeremiah lived at the time of the beginning of the Babylonian exile in 587 B.C.E. Jeremiah is speaking to the Jews in Babylon. The prophet foretells the coming of a new covenant between Yahweh and God's people, a superior and more spiritual one written in the hearts of the people. The old covenant has been broken, rendered null and void by the widespread disloyalty of the people to its stipulations. In particular, they broke the oath of loyalty to Yahweh by worshiping other gods, especially the nature god Baal, the god of the Canaanites.

The context of Jeremiah's prophecy is either to the people of the northern kingdom of Israel after they had been exiled to Assyria, or to the exilic people of the southern kingdom of Judah after Jerusalem had fallen and many had been exiled to Babylonia. If the former, then the text of Jeremiah 31:31-34 originated in the mid-seventh century B.C.E., but if the latter is the historical context, our passage was composed shortly after 586 B.C.E. In whatever context, the people heard themselves addressed as a people who had violated the covenant, who had not been faithful and had been punished for their unfaithfulness. Yet, Jeremiah assured them that God remained faithful and would forgive the Israelites for their idolatry, would write the divine will upon their hearts, and would renew the broken bond of communion.

In what ways would it be like the Sinai covenant? In what ways would it be different? Jeremiah knew that laws do not change human beings. Josiah's reforms had changed outward practices but the Israelites' hearts remained selfish and they soon learned how to adapt any outward law or ritual to serve their self-interest.

60

God promises to make a new covenant with Israel and Judah because they had abused the Mosaic covenant by turning it into a business deal in which they promised to do certain outward deeds in return for God's favor. Their lives are changed, however, when they know God, accept God's love in their hearts, and respond to that love. That is what Jeremiah envisioned.

In Jeremiah 31:33-34, a new and better covenant is promised by God. The promise, "I will be their God and they will be my people" (Exod. 6:7; Deut. 7:6; 10:15; 26:18), is now renewed by Jeremiah (31:33). The context seems to imply that the sin of Israel is so great until God has to intervene in a mighty way. Persons are to be made new, but not by new and better laws and rituals written on stone tablets. Now the covenant is to become so deeply a part of each person that there will no longer be a need for teaching. When God is known in their hearts, that relationship affects and transforms everything done. There is natural and spontaneous obedience to God's laws when the heart is made new. The message of hope that Jeremiah offers is that there can be a transformed world when people know and respond to God through a transformed heart.

Here we revisit the symbol in Ash Wednesday's reading from Joel that depicted "tearing of the heart" as a sign of repentance and renewal. Sincerity and true repentance bridge the gap caused by Israel's refusal to live up to the covenant.

SECOND LESSON: HEBREWS 5:7-10

The Epistle to the Hebrews alternates between ethical exhortation and theological exposition, the one reinforcing the other. Hebrews 5:1—10:18 argues that Jesus is superior to the priesthood and the priestly work of Aaron. This major theological theme of Christ as the heavenly high priest is dealt with mainly in chapter 7, but the author prepares the ground for this in the prior chapters. The author intends to first show that although Jesus is not of Levitical descent, he was indeed a high priest, one of the order of Melchizedek, a theme he enunciates several times before he develops it. Our present passage is placed between two such pronouncements (vv. 5-6, 10). The author argues that a priest is one like ourselves, who bears our infirmities, weaknesses, and petitions before God. All priests were human beings who were made holy and sacred by virtue of their work. This was true of Aaron and of every priest, but, our author argues, it is even more true of Jesus Christ (5:5, 6).

In 5:7-10, the author wishes to prove that Jesus Christ has the necessary qualifications for high priest. He does this by arguing that no high priest appoints himself to the office, but is chosen by God. This is illustrated by referring to Christ's Gethsemane scene. Christ did not seek honors for himself at Gethsemane, but gave himself over completely to the will of God. The Gethsemane prayer was heard, but this does not mean that Jesus was saved from death, as he prayed: "Father, let this cup pass from me." Rather, through death and resurrection, Jesus was made perfect. God brought Jesus to perfection. Even if Jesus were morally perfect, the work of Christ does not merely connote moral perfection. We are told in Hebrews that Jesus was in all points tempted as we, but he was yet without sin.

Perfect means reaching a goal or destiny. In the case of Jesus, his destiny was to become our perfect high priest. To this office he was divinely appointed at the resurrection. Jesus, therefore, becomes the source of divine salvation to all who accept the gospel. Jesus is a priest because of two essential things: He has a divine appointment (5:1), and he has true humanity (5:5, 8).

One of the most powerful statements is that our Savior is one like us, one tempted like us, yet above it all. This is the good news—Jesus does not have to have my experiences to understand my pain and need. Reverend Barbara Essex, a minister in the United Church of Christ and my colleague at Hartford Seminary, gave a sermon for a womanist event in which she depicted the divine humanness of Jesus:

> Our God opens our eyes to see wells of water, hope in desert wilderness places and experiences. Our God through Jesus Christ assures us that help is on the way. We turn to Jesus not because we need a man to rescue us; we turn to Jesus because he understands! Jesus is not a Black woman, but he knows what it means to be gifted and have those gifts rejected by his own people. Jesus is not a Black woman, but he knows what it means to be scorned and abandoned by those closest to him. Jesus is not a Black woman, but he knows what it means to be misunderstood and silenced by those in power. Jesus is not a Black woman, but he knows what it means to be scared. Jesus is not a Black woman, but he knows what it means to be an outcast. Jesus is not a Black woman, but he knows what it means to be betrayed. Jesus is not a Black woman, but he knows what it means to be despised. Jesus is not a Black woman,

but he knows what it means to be denied a ministry. Jesus is not a Black woman, but he knows what it means to suffer. Jesus is not a Black woman, but he knows what it means to be beaten and mocked and stereotyped. Jesus is not a Black woman but he knows what it means to be resurrected!

Sisters, despite all that the world has dealt us, still we rise! God sends one who knows what we feel and experience, God sends God's Holy Spirit to raise us up over and over and over again.

We have a high priest who has become our savior because of his identification with our basic needs. For this relationship, we are thankful. What is said above about women, can be repeated by all who have their backs against the wall.

GOSPEL: JOHN 12:20-33

In John 9, the hostility of Jewish leaders is portrayed in narrative form, as they refuse to draw the proper inferences from Jesus' restoration of sight to the blind man. John 10, in which Jesus speaks of himself as the good shepherd, again eventuates in a heated controversy. The raising of Lazarus, God's restoration of life through Jesus (John 11), leads to a firm decision for Jesus' death on the part of his opponents (11:45-53). After a brief withdrawal from public view (11:54), Jesus once again goes to Jerusalem (John 12), enters the city triumphantly (12:12-19), and makes a series of pronouncements, his last public utterances before his death.

While we are not told that they got to see Jesus, the appearance of some Greeks seeking him (12:20) doubtless prefigures the spread of the good news about him beyond Judaism, and his Jewish enemies to the Greco-Roman world. "The hour" of the cross for John is the total meaning and fulfillment of Jesus' mission. This theme is developed by the statement, "Unless a grain of wheat falls into the ground and dies, it remains just a single grain; but if it dies, it bears much fruit" (12:24). Jesus cannot flee the way of the cross if a new humanity is to take place (12:23-26). This sentiment is summed up in the last statement of Jesus in the presence of the crowd (12:27-33), especially verse 32: "And I, when I am lifted up from the earth, will draw all people to myself."

In his humanity Jesus trembles as crucifixion approaches. At the same time, Jesus affirms his will to press forward toward this "hour"

(v. 27). It is the hour of the glory of the Abba achieved in full manifestation of the love of the Son. "The ruler of this world," who will celebrate this death as a victory, will in reality have sealed his defeat: The order of oppression stands judged and condemned (v. 31).

The answer to the Greek's statement to Philip, "We wish to see Jesus"—that is, to experience messianic salvation—is in the negative. They cannot see Jesus because Gentiles were not the earthly focus of Jesus' ministry on this side of the crucifixion. Post-resurrection manifestation would be prevalent when the Jew could no longer boast of their law and the Gentile could no longer refuse reconciliation to the Jews. This would be effected through the cross of Christ that broke down the dividing wall of partition and made the field level for both Jew and Gentile. The Gentile will then be able to "see" or experience the messianic salvation through the cross of Christ.

We have come full circle: Our journey has a completion to it. We have moved from anonymity to being known by God; we have moved from chaotic selfishness to covenant and community; we have moved from waywardness to renewal; we have moved from doubt to hope. We have wrestled with angels and have been tempted in the wilderness. We have argued our faith, backed down, and almost given up. Jesus yet stands at the threshold of our being. He requires an answer from us: Are we for him or against him? Lent provides the time and the space to answer. Thanks be to God!